"This series is a tremendous resource for tl
understanding of how the gospel is wovei
pastors and scholars doing gospel business
logical feast preparing God's people to appl,
wholly committed to Christ's priorities."

> **BRYAN CHAPELL,** President Emeritus, Covenant Theological Seminary; Senior Pastor, Grace Presbyterian Church, Peoria, Illinois

"Mark Twain may have smiled when he wrote to a friend, 'I didn't have time to write you a short letter, so I wrote you a long letter.' But the truth of Twain's remark remains serious and universal, because well-reasoned, compact writing requires extra time and extra hard work. And this is what we have in the Crossway Bible study series *Knowing the Bible*. The skilled authors and notable editors provide the contours of each book of the Bible as well as the grand theological themes that bind them together as one Book. Here, in a 12-week format, are carefully wrought studies that will ignite the mind and the heart."

> **R. KENT HUGHES,** Visiting Professor of Practical Theology, Westminster Theological Seminary

"*Knowing the Bible* brings together a gifted team of Bible teachers to produce a high-quality series of study guides. The coordinated focus of these materials is unique: biblical content, provocative questions, systematic theology, practical application, and the gospel story of God's grace presented all the way through Scripture."

> **PHILIP G. RYKEN,** President, Wheaton College

"These *Knowing the Bible* volumes provide a significant and very welcome variation on the general run of inductive Bible studies. This series provides substantial instruction, as well as teaching through the very questions that are asked. *Knowing the Bible* then goes even further by showing how any given text links with the gospel, the whole Bible, and the formation of theology. I heartily endorse this orientation of individual books to the whole Bible and the gospel, and I applaud the demonstration that sound theology was not something invented later by Christians, but is right there in the pages of Scripture."

> **GRAEME L. GOLDSWORTHY,** former lecturer, Moore Theological College; author, *According to Plan, Gospel and Kingdom, The Gospel in Revelation*, and *Gospel and Wisdom*

"What a gift to earnest, Bible-loving, Bible-searching believers! The organization and structure of the Bible study format presented through the *Knowing the Bible* series is so well conceived. Students of the Word are led to understand the content of passages through perceptive, guided questions, and they are given rich insights and application all along the way in the brief but illuminating sections that conclude each study. What potential growth in depth and breadth of understanding these studies offer! One can only pray that vast numbers of believers will discover more of God and the beauty of his Word through these rich studies."

> **BRUCE A. WARE,** Professor of Christian Theology, The Southern Baptist Theological Seminary

KNOWING THE BIBLE

J. I. Packer, Theological Editor
Dane C. Ortlund, Series Editor
Lane T. Dennis, Executive Editor

•   •   •   •   •   •

Genesis	Psalms	John	1–2 Thessalonians
Exodus	Proverbs	Acts	1–2 Timothy
Leviticus	Ecclesiastes	Romans	and Titus
Deuteronomy	Isaiah	1 Corinthians	Hebrews
Joshua	Jeremiah	2 Corinthians	James
Ruth and Esther	Daniel	Galatians	1–2 Peter
1–2 Kings	Hosea	Ephesians	and Jude
Ezra and	Matthew	Philippians	Revelation
Nehemiah	Mark	Colossians and	
Job	Luke	Philemon	

•   •   •   •   •   •

J. I. PACKER is Board of Governors' Professor of Theology at Regent College (Vancouver, BC). Dr. Packer earned his DPhil at the University of Oxford. He is known and loved worldwide as the author of the best-selling book *Knowing God*, as well as many other titles on theology and the Christian life. He serves as the General Editor of the ESV Bible and as the Theological Editor for the *ESV Study Bible*.

LANE T. DENNIS is President of Crossway, a not-for-profit publishing ministry. Dr. Dennis earned his PhD from Northwestern University. He is Chair of the ESV Bible Translation Oversight Committee and Executive Editor of the *ESV Study Bible*.

DANE C. ORTLUND is Executive Vice President of Bible Publishing and Bible Publisher at Crossway. He is a graduate of Covenant Theological Seminary (MDiv, ThM) and Wheaton College (BA, PhD). Dr. Ortlund has authored several books and scholarly articles in the areas of Bible, theology, and Christian living.

1–2 KINGS

A 12-WEEK STUDY

Gavin Ortlund

WHEATON, ILLINOIS

Knowing the Bible: 1–2 Kings, A 12-Week Study

Copyright © 2017 by Crossway

Published by Crossway
    1300 Crescent Street
    Wheaton, Illinois 60187

Some content used in this study guide has been adapted from the *ESV Study Bible* (Crossway), copyright 2008 by Crossway, pages 585–695. Used by permission. All rights reserved.

Cover design: Simplicated Studio

First printing 2017

Printed in the United States of America

Trade paperback ISBN: 978-1-4335-5370-7
EPub ISBN: 978-1-4335-5373-8
PDF ISBN: 978-1-4335-5371-4
Mobipocket ISBN: 978-1-4335-5372-1

Crossway is a publishing ministry of Good News Publishers.

VP		28	27	26	25	24	23	22	21	20	19	18	17
15	14	13	12	11	10	9	8	7	6	5	4	3	2	1

TABLE OF CONTENTS

SERIES PREFACE

KNOWING THE BIBLE, as the series title indicates, was created to help readers know and understand the meaning, the message, and the God of the Bible. Each volume in the series consists of 12 units that progressively take the reader through a clear, concise study of that book of the Bible. In this way, any given volume can fruitfully be used in a 12-week format either in group study, such as in a church-based context, or in individual study. Of course, these 12 studies could be completed in fewer or more than 12 weeks, as convenient, depending on the context in which they are used.

Each study unit gives an overview of the text at hand before digging into it with a series of questions for reflection or discussion. The unit then concludes by highlighting the gospel of grace in each passage ("Gospel Glimpses"), identifying whole-Bible themes that occur in the passage ("Whole-Bible Connections"), and pinpointing Christian doctrines that are affirmed in the passage ("Theological Soundings").

The final component to each unit is a section for reflecting on personal and practical implications from the passage at hand. The layout provides space for recording responses to the questions proposed, and we think readers need to do this to get the full benefit of the exercise. The series also includes definitions of key words. These definitions are indicated by a note number in the text and are found at the end of each chapter.

Lastly, to help understand the Bible in this deeper way, we urge readers to use the ESV Bible and the *ESV Study Bible,* which are available in various print and digital formats, including online editions at esv.org. The Knowing the Bible series is also available online. Additional 12-week studies covering each book of the Bible will be added as they become available.

May the Lord greatly bless your study as you seek to know him through knowing his Word.

J. I. Packer

Lane T. Dennis

WEEK 1: OVERVIEW

Getting Acquainted

The books of 1 and 2 Kings tell a sad story. The narrative begins at the height of the Israelite monarchy, as Solomon inherits the kingdom of his father, David, and goes on to acquire his own vast wealth and fame. The story ends in utter devastation, as the remaining people of the dwindling southern kingdom of Judah are carried off to Babylon in exile.[1] There are a few bright spots along the way—the prophetic ministry of Elijah/Elisha, for instance, as well as Hezekiah's prayer for miraculous deliverance and the reforms under Josiah—but the overall trajectory of the narrative seems to plunge inexorably downward.

Yet this very pattern helps to express the meaning of the books of Kings. First and Second Kings do not merely describe a litany of decline and judgment; they highlight God's working amid that decline to fulfill his program of redemption. In the structure of 1–2 Kings, we detect a faint shadow of the gospel story itself, which arrives at resurrection only through the slow, grinding agony of crucifixion. As we consider God's work in 1–2 Kings, we will gain a better sense of his plan to advance his purposes through all the frustrations and failures of life.

First and Second Kings display God's enduring faithfulness, amid great opposition and against all appearance, through temple,[2] covenant,[3] prophetic oracle,[4] reform, and—when all other hope has faded—the coming Davidic King. (For further background, see the *ESV Study Bible*, pages 585–590; available online at esv.org.)

Placing 1–2 Kings in the Larger Story

As the era of 1–2 Kings begins, God has delivered his people from Egypt, given them his law, and led them into the land he had promised to them. They have seen their need for a leader, and God has raised up David (over Saul) as their king. The books of 1–2 Kings narrate the history of God's people during the period of the monarchy, picking up after 1–2 Samuel, which ended at the conclusion of David's reign. With its emphasis on the sin and idolatry of God's people and its concluding reference to the continuation of the Davidic line (2 Kings 25:27–30), the story of 1–2 Kings shows the need for Jesus Christ, the promised Davidic ruler who would usher in God's kingdom and lead God's people in righteousness.

Key Verse

"This occurred because the people of Israel had sinned against the LORD their God, who had brought them up out of the land of Egypt from under the hand of Pharaoh king of Egypt, and had feared other gods and walked in the customs of the nations whom the LORD drove out before the people of Israel, and in the customs that the kings of Israel had practiced." (2 Kings 17:7–8)

Date and Historical Background

First and Second Kings were written sometime after the destruction of Jerusalem in 586 BC. They must have been completed sometime after 561 BC, because the books' final verses recount King Jehoiachin's release from prison in that year. No one knows their exact date of composition, or the identity of their author(s). Many scholars believe that earlier material was used in the construction of these books, and it is also possible that the books underwent later editing following their initial composition.

The books of 1–2 Kings were written, in part, in order to demonstrate that the exile of God's people was a judgment of God on the people's persistence in idolatry. Much of 1–2 Kings reflects the language and theology of the book of Deuteronomy, emphasizing that God's judgment had come as the promised result of disobedience to his law.

Outline

  I. The Reign of Solomon (1 Kings 1:1–11:43)
    A. Solomon acquires the throne (1 Kings 1:1–2:46)
    B. Solomon asks for wisdom (1 Kings 3:1–4:34)
    C. The temple is built and dedicated (1 Kings 5:1–8:66)

As You Get Started

Do you have a sense at the outset of this study of any specific themes in 1 or 2 Kings? Are there any stories from these books that have particularly stood out to you in the past? How would you summarize the contributions you believe that 1–2 Kings makes to the message of the entire Bible?

What is your current understanding of what 1–2 Kings contributes to Christian theology? That is, how do these books clarify our understanding of God, Jesus Christ, sin, salvation, the end times, or other doctrines?

What aspects of 1 or 2 Kings have confused you? Are there any specific questions you hope to have answered through this study?

> ## As You Finish This Unit . . .

Take a few minutes to ask God to bless you with increased understanding and a transformed heart and life as you begin this study of 1–2 Kings.

Definitions

[1] **Exile** – Several relocations of large groups of Israelites/Jews have occurred throughout history, but "the exile" typically refers to the Babylonian exile, that is, Nebuchadnezzar's relocation of residents of the southern kingdom of Judah to Babylon in 586 BC. (Residents of the northern kingdom of Israel had been resettled by Assyria in 722 BC.) After Babylon came under Persian rule, several waves of Jewish exiles returned and repopulated Judah.

[2] **Temple** – A place set aside as holy because of God's presence there. Solomon built the first temple of the Lord in Jerusalem, to replace the portable tabernacle. This temple was later destroyed by the Babylonians, rebuilt, and destroyed again by the Romans.

[3] **Covenant** – A binding agreement between two parties, typically involving a formal statement of their relationship, a list of stipulations and obligations for both parties, a list of witnesses to the agreement, and a list of curses for unfaithfulness and blessings for faithfulness to the agreement. The OT is more properly understood as the old covenant, meaning the agreement established between God and his people prior to the coming of Jesus Christ and the establishment of the new covenant (NT).

[4] **Oracle** – From Latin "to speak." In the Bible, this term refers to a divine pronouncement delivered through a human agent.

WEEK 2: THE WEALTH AND WISDOM OF SOLOMON

1 Kings 1:1–4:34

The Place of the Passage

First Kings picks up where 2 Samuel left off: at the conclusion of King David's reign. First Kings 1–4 recounts Solomon's rise to the throne and early accomplishments. In chapter 1, Solomon is anointed king, despite the threat of Adonijah, in fulfillment of God's promise to David in 2 Samuel 7:12–13. In chapter 2, after a final charge from David, Solomon's reign is fully established. In chapter 3, Solomon asks the Lord for wisdom, which God grants him, along with riches and honor. Chapter 4 describes a season of blessing, prosperity, and peace among God's people under Solomon's reign.

The Big Picture

First Kings 1–4 demonstrates God's faithfulness to his promises, his responsiveness to prayer, and his blessings upon obedience.

> ### Reflection and Discussion

Read through the complete passage for this study, 1 Kings 1–4. Then review the questions below concerning this introductory section of 1 Kings and write your notes on them. (For further background, see the *ESV Study Bible*, pages 591–601; available online at esv.org.)

1. Solomon's Acquisition of the Throne (1 Kings 1–2)

Why do you think 1 Kings 1–2 is in the Bible? The narrative could simply have skipped from the end of David's reign in 2 Samuel 24 to Solomon's request for wisdom in 1 Kings 3, or at least it could have compressed much of the details and drama of these two lengthy chapters (99 verses). None of the later kings in the book, for instance, see their arrival on the throne described at such length. What do these chapters add to the narrative? Where do you see God's activity and faithfulness in these chapters? (Consider, e.g., 1 Kings 1:29–30 or 2:45–46.)

First Kings 1:5 records that Adonijah "exalted himself," aspiring to be king. Solomon, by contrast, is relatively inactive—his selection as king comes about largely through the efforts of Nathan and Bathsheba (1:11–27). What can we learn about God's sovereignty[1] in this passage (see, e.g., 2:15)? Are there any ways in which the events of 1 Kings 1–2 might serve as an illustration of Jesus' words in Luke 14:11?

In David's final charge to Solomon, he exhorts his son both to righteous character (2:1–4) and to the execution of justice (2:5–9). What do you think Christians today should learn from this charge? In what ways (if any) do you think this charge was unique to Solomon as king over God's people?

2. Solomon's Wisdom and Blessing (1 Kings 3–4)

According to 3:7–9, why does Solomon ask for wisdom? What do you think is going on in Solomon's heart as he makes this request?

It pleases the Lord that Solomon asks for wisdom (3:10). What does God commend Solomon for *not* asking for (e.g., in 3:11, 13)? Why do you think wisdom is superior to these things, in God's sight?

In 1 Kings 3:16–28, Solomon's wisdom is demonstrated through the narrative of two prostitutes who come to him with a dispute. Why do you think the author included this story? What is the *purpose* of Solomon's wisdom, as it functions here (see, e.g., 3:28)?

All of chapter 3 reflects a very high estimation of the value of wisdom. In what ways is wisdom as portrayed in this chapter different from mere intelligence? How is wisdom as portrayed here dependent upon humility and faith? You may want to consider Proverbs 1:7 and James 1:5–8 as you reflect upon this question.

Chapter 4 describes a sort of "golden age" among God's people in which, under Solomon's rule, "Judah and Israel were as many as the sand by the sea. They ate and drank and were happy" (4:20). This initial season of prosperity stands out in contrast with the rest of the book as a reminder that God is eager to bless his people when they walk in his ways (as he promises, e.g., in 2:1–4, 3:13–14). What strikes you as most impressive in the account of Solomon's officials, possessions, and wisdom in 1 Kings 4? What does this chapter reveal about God's character?

First Kings 4:34 records that "the people of all nations came to hear the wisdom of Solomon." God has always been concerned with advancing his purposes among all the nations of the earth (see Gen. 12:3). How does the fame of Solomon's wisdom depict the missional nature of the Israelite monarchy? How do you think the world might be different today if Israel's kings had been consistently obedient?

Read through the following three sections on *Gospel Glimpses*, *Whole-Bible Connections*, and *Theological Soundings*. Then take time to consider the *Personal Implications* these sections may have for you.

Gospel Glimpses

GOD'S PEOPLE NEED A KING. All throughout 1–2 Kings, God's people share in blessing when a good king follows the Lord and share in judgment when an evil king rejects the Lord. As goes the leader, so goes the entire nation. This is one of the most basic implications of how 1–2 Kings is structured—as a succession of kings in which the fate of the people is bound up with the integrity of their leader. In 1 Kings 1–2, God is faithful to provide his people with a king, the promised offspring of David. Tragically, both this king and most of those who follow him will ultimately let the people down by disobeying the Lord. But in the larger story of the whole Bible, of which 1–2 Kings is just one chapter, God provides the perfect King, the promised descendant of David whose obedience brings salvation and blessing to the whole world. As we read through story after story of failed kings in 1–2 Kings, we see the depth of our need for this King, and we long for his arrival.

GOD'S EAGERNESS TO BLESS HIS PEOPLE. First and Second Kings have much to say about divine judgment,[2] as does much of the rest of the Old Testament. Sometimes the God of the Old Testament is caricatured as a knee-jerk, tempestuous person who is always smiting people. In reality, the deepest heart of God, from Genesis to Revelation, is love. In this portion of Scripture, especially 1 Kings 3–4, we see God's responsiveness to the prayers of his people and his eagerness to bless them as they seek his face and walk in his ways. Christ's lament in Matthew 23:37 reflects this same disposition in God's heart toward blessing his people: "O Jerusalem, Jerusalem, the city that kills the prophets and stones those who are sent to it! How often would I have gathered your children together as a hen gathers her brood under her wings, and you were not willing." In the work of Christ, which is the clearest revelation of the heart of God for his people, we find a God who not only is *eager* to bless his people but who spares no expense to bless them, even at the cost of his Son's very life.

Whole-Bible Connections

DAVIDIC COVENANT. In 2 Samuel 7:12–16, God had promised David that one of his offspring would rule on his throne, that he would build a house for God, and that God would establish his kingdom forever. First Kings 1–2 establishes God's fulfillment of this promise with the accession of Solomon, who will eventually build the temple (1 Kings 5–8). Nonetheless, Solomon's disobedience leads to the Lord's discipline and the division of the nation (see 1 Kings 11:9–13). Ultimately, 1–2 Kings leaves the reader with an expectation of a future Davidic King who will usher in an everlasting kingdom and rule over God's people in righteousness. In the New Testament, the apostles proclaim Jesus Christ as this promised Davidic King, and his resurrection and ascension to heaven function as his royal enthronement (e.g., Acts 2:29–36, 13:32–37). Today Jesus is reigning from his heavenly throne and advancing his kingdom, and one day he will return to consummate his everlasting kingdom in the new heaven and new earth.

SACRIFICE AND ARK. In 1 Kings 3:4, just before the Lord appears to Solomon, the king offers burnt offerings at Gibeon. Then, after his dream, he returns to Jerusalem to stand before the ark of covenant, offering both burnt offerings and peace offerings (3:15). These are two of the five major kinds of offerings prescribed in Leviticus 1–7 (for further exploration of these various sacrifices, see the *ESV Study Bible*, pages 217–225). Each of these sacrifices served a specific function among God's people, but the overarching purpose of the sacrificial system was to prepare God's people for the ultimate sacrifice of Christ, who fulfilled them all (Heb. 10:1–18). The ark of the covenant was constructed along with the tabernacle[3] in Exodus 25–31; on top of it was a lid called the mercy seat. The ark was kept in the Most Holy Place and symbolized God's enthroned presence among his people. Each year, on the Day of Atonement,[4] the high priest would enter the Most Holy Place and sprinkle the blood of animals on the mercy seat in order to atone for the sins of God's people. This ritual also pointed to, and was fulfilled by, the sacrifice of Christ (see, e.g., Heb. 9:1–14). In the next section of 1 Kings we will see the ark brought into the temple at the temple's dedication (1 Kings 8:1–11).

Theological Soundings

SIN AND JUDGMENT. Because of his holy and righteous character, God must punish sin. In this portion of God's Word we find numerous instances of people's sin catching up with them, with judgment being meted out by God's leaders as a result. In 1 Kings 2:5–9, David exhorts Solomon to execute justice upon Joab and Shimei for their treacherous behavior during David's reign. Throughout 2:13–46, Solomon deals with these characters and others, instructing Benaiah to strike down Joab and Adonijah, expelling Abiathar, and confining Shimei to Jerusalem (later Shimei ignores this instruction and is also struck down by Benaiah). A cynical reader might regard this as the vindictive behavior of a newly established king who seeks to consolidate his power. However, we must recognize that it is right to punish sin, and within the context of the Israelite theocracy God used human agents as mediators of his judgment.

GOD'S SOVEREIGNTY IN BESTOWING GIFTS. Throughout 1 Kings 1–4 God sovereignly bestows good gifts to Solomon, including vast wealth and wisdom and even the promise to prolong his years (3:14). In these chapters we are reminded that all good gifts are distributed ultimately by God, including the very length of our life. As James 1:17 puts it, "Every good gift and every perfect gift"—whether organizational skill (1 Kings 4:1–19) or the knowledge of trees and animals (4:33)—"is from above."

OBEDIENCE AND BLESSING. God is pleased with Solomon's request for wisdom and his desire to rule justly over God's people (1 Kings 3:10). Solomon's wisdom results in a season of great prosperity and blessing among God's people (e.g., 4:20). Sometimes well-meaning Christians, seeking to emphasize the determinative role of God's grace in orienting our relationship with him, downplay the role of obedience in the life of the Christian, as if all efforts at obedience were inherently legalistic. This story reminds us that, while we cannot earn God's favor through our obedience, our efforts at obedience, in response to the grace of God given to us in the gospel, bring pleasure to our heavenly Father and result in his blessing.

> ## Personal Implications

Take time to reflect on the implications of 1 Kings 1–4 for your own life today. Make notes below on the personal implications for your walk with the Lord of the (1) *Gospel Glimpses*, (2) *Whole-Bible Connections*, (3) *Theological Soundings*, and (4) this passage as a whole.

1. Gospel Glimpses

2. Whole-Bible Connections

3. Theological Soundings

4. 1 Kings 1:1–4:34

As You Finish This Unit . . .

Take a moment now to ask for the Lord's blessing and help as you continue in this study of 1 Kings. And take a moment also to look back through this unit of study, to reflect on some key things that the Lord may be teaching you.

Definitions

[1] **Sovereignty** – Supreme and independent power and authority. Sovereignty over all things is a distinctive attribute of God (1 Tim. 6:15–16). He directs all things for his own purposes (Rom. 8:28–29).

[2] **Judgment** – Any assessment of something or someone, especially moral assessment. The Bible speaks of a final day of judgment when Christ will return to judge all those who have refused to repent (Rev. 20:12–15).

[3] **Tabernacle** – The tent where God dwelled on earth and communed with his people as Israel's divine King. Also referred to as the "tent of meeting" (Lev. 1:5), this structure was later replaced by the temple in Jerusalem.

[4] **Day of Atonement** – The holiest day in the Israelite calendar, on which atonement was made for all the sins of Israel from the past year (Leviticus 16). It occurred on the tenth day of the seventh month (September/October), and all Israel was to fast and do no work. Only on that day each year could someone—the high priest—enter the Most Holy Place of the tabernacle (later, the temple) and offer the necessary sacrifices. A "scapegoat" would also be sent into the wilderness as a sign of Israel's sins being carried away.

WEEK 3: THE TEMPLE: GOD'S PRESENCE AMONG HIS PEOPLE

1 Kings 5:1–10:29

▲

The Place of the Passage

These chapters chronicle Solomon's construction of the temple, which includes a detailed account of its furnishings (7:13–51) and culminates in Solomon's lengthy prayer of dedication as the ark is brought into the temple (8:22–61). In response to Solomon's prayer, God promises his presence among his people, mediated through the temple: "My eyes and my heart will be there for all time" (9:3). Solomon's renowned wisdom and wealth are further described, although there are disturbing hints that his wealth may be pulling his heart away from the Lord. For example, it is curious that he spends more time building his own palace than building the Lord's temple (see 7:1–12). The conclusion of this section thus prepares the reader for Solomon's turning away from the Lord, and its tragic results for the rest of God's people, in the chapters that follow.

The Big Picture

In 1 Kings 5–10, Solomon leads in the preparation, building, and dedication of the temple, and God promises that his presence will dwell there.

Read through the complete passage for this study, 1 Kings 5–10. Then review the questions below concerning this section of 1 Kings and write your notes on them. (For further background, see the *ESV Study Bible*, pages 601–617; available online at esv.org.)

1. Preparation and Construction of the Temple (1 Kings 5–7)

First Kings 5:1–12 recounts Solomon's treaty with Hiram, king of Tyre, who provided Solomon with timber for the construction of the temple. First Kings 5:13–18 describes the organization and oversight of Solomon's workforce. Why do you think this chapter is in the Bible? Taking these two sections of the chapter together, how do you see this chapter fitting in with, and contributing to, the surrounding narrative concerning Solomon's wisdom and the construction of the temple?

First Kings 6–7 describes the actual building of the temple, relating its timeline and physical details. Why was it important for the author to record the exact size and proportions of the interior of the temple? According to Hebrews 9:1–10, what was the purpose of the physical structures of the tabernacle/temple (e.g., the curtain)?

The detailed description of the temple is interrupted briefly by God's promise to Solomon in 1 Kings 6:11–13, which sets the temple construction in the larger theological context of Israel's covenant relationship with the Lord. According to these verses, what is the purpose of the temple?

2. Temple Dedication (1 Kings 8)

Solomon's initial prayer of blessing (8:12–21) sets the temple within the larger context of the exodus[1] (Moses) and the monarchy (David). How, according to Solomon's prayer, does the temple serve as the fulfillment of this larger history?

Make a list of the four or five biggest requests in Solomon's prayer in 8:22–61. What themes stand out to you in this prayer?

Solomon's closing benediction brings his prayer to a climax by emphasizing the missional nature of God's covenant relationship with Israel: "that all the peoples of the earth may know that the LORD is God; there is no other" (8:60). We normally do not think of the temple as serving a missional purpose, but how do you think God desired the surrounding Gentile nations to view the temple? As you consider your answer, you may want to observe the similar sensitivity to non-Israelites in 8:41–43.

3. Solomon's Other Activity (1 Kings 9–10)

How is the Lord's second appearance to Solomon (9:1–9) similar to his first (3:1–5)? How is it different? How would you describe the purpose of this second appearance?

In the remainder of this chapter (9:10–28), the account of Solomon's activity after the construction of the temple and his palace picks up on several themes from chapter 5—particularly his treaty with Hiram and his use of forced labor. As you read this portion of the text, do you sense any hints of imperfection or suspicion regarding Solomon's character?

First Kings 10 records yet another detailed account of Solomon's wealth and wisdom, similar to previous accounts in, for instance, 1 Kings 3–4. Why do you think Solomon's wisdom and wealth were important enough to repeat in detail? What do you think was the *purpose* of Solomon's wisdom and wealth, in relation to the other theological themes of the book (obedience, temple, Davidic covenant, etc.)? What was the Queen of Sheba's impression of the God of Israel as a result of Solomon's wisdom and wealth?

Read through the following three sections on *Gospel Glimpses*, *Whole-Bible Connections*, and *Theological Soundings*. Then take time to consider the *Personal Implications* these sections may have for you.

> ## Gospel Glimpses

FORGIVENESS OF SINS. In his prayer of dedication for the temple, Solomon prays that God would hear his people's prayers for forgiveness of sins as they pray in the temple (1 Kings 8:31–53). Solomon envisions six different scenarios in which people would need forgiveness when praying in the temple (wrongdoing resulting in a legal case, military defeat, famine, a foreigner praying to the God of Israel, God's people going to battle, and sin resulting in exile). The root need in each scenario is the need to deal with sin, and Solomon's prayer reflects sensitivity to the need that God's people have for ongoing forgiveness in their lives. In the new covenant era, we have continual forgiveness through Christ's intercession for us (1 John 2:1) and thus we have confidence to enter into his presence and have our guilty consciences washed clean (Heb. 10:19–22).

GOD'S COVENANT FAITHFULNESS. The faithfulness of God to his covenant promises is a recurring theme throughout this portion of Scripture. In Solomon's prayer at the temple dedication, for instance, he begins by affirming God's uniqueness in contrast to the gods of other nations as a covenant-keeping God: "There is no God like you, in heaven above or on earth beneath, keeping covenant and showing steadfast love to your servants who walk before you with all their heart" (8:23). Throughout these chapters, more clearly than in most other books of the Old Testament, we find God's various covenants interwoven, as the construction of God's temple is cast in relation to the fulfillment of the Davidic covenant (6:12; 8:15–20; 9:5), the exodus from Egypt (8:16, 53), and God's concern to bless all the nations of the earth through his people (8:41–43, 59–60; compare Gen. 12:3). The temple is therefore part of the fulfillment of the Davidic, Mosaic, and Abrahamic covenants and thus calls for reciprocal covenant faithfulness among God's people, to walk in his ways and keep his statutes (1 Kings 6:12; 8:58; 9:4). Ultimately, however, the fulfillment of these covenants, as well as the purpose of the temple, would occur with the coming of Christ, the very "temple" of God, dwelling among us in bodily form (John 1:14; 2:19), who would sit on the throne of David, free God's people from the slavery of sin, and spread God's blessings to all the nations of the earth.

Whole-Bible Connections

THE CLOUD OF GLORY. Throughout the Old Testament, God's glory is often associated with the appearance of a cloud (e.g., Ex. 16:10). This cloud often appears as a manifestation of God's presence and guidance in connection to the tabernacle/temple. After the ark is brought into the temple, 1 Kings 8:10–11 records that "a cloud filled the house of the LORD, so that the priests could not stand to minister because of the cloud, for the glory of the LORD filled the house of the LORD." This recalls a strikingly similar occurrence upon the completion of the *tabernacle* in Exodus 40:34–35: "Then the cloud covered the tent of meeting, and the glory of the LORD filled the tabernacle. And Moses was not able to enter the tent of meeting because the cloud settled on it, and the glory of the LORD filled the tabernacle." First Kings 8:10–11 thus indicates continuity between God's glorious presence at Sinai and over the tabernacle (Ex. 40:36–38) and his glorious presence now in the temple. In the New Testament, Christ's transfiguration (Luke 9:34), ascension (Acts 1:9), and second coming (1 Thess. 4:17) are also associated with a cloud of glory.

GOD'S DWELLING AMONG HIS PEOPLE. Adam and Eve enjoyed God's direct presence in Eden, before sin entered the world. Ever since the rupturing of that relationship as a result of sin, God has been reestablishing his presence among his people, first through the tabernacle, then through the temple, and finally through Christ, who is himself the temple of God (John 2:21) and whose death tore open the curtain separating us from God (Matt. 27:51; Heb. 10:20). He makes us into his temple through the Holy Spirit (1 Cor. 3:16). In heaven, we will again enjoy the direct presence of God as he dwells among his people (Rev. 21:3). The detailed proportions of the temple given in 1 Kings 6–7, similar to those of the tabernacle described in Exodus 25–31 and to those of the new temple described in Ezekiel 40–48, point to this deeper thread throughout the entire Bible of God's desire to dwell among his people.

Theological Soundings

OBEDIENCE VERSUS DISOBEDIENCE. Solomon's dedicatory prayer emphasizes that God blesses obedience and punishes disobedience (e.g., 1 Kings 8:31–32). The greatest Old Testament example of this truth is the exile, ominously hinted at in 8:46–53. Throughout these chapters of 1 Kings this theme is sounded repeatedly—for instance, at the climax of the Lord's second appearance to Solomon (9:4–9) and in his earlier instruction to Solomon in 6:11–13. The motif of blessing for obedience and cursing for disobedience recalls Deuteronomy 28, and 1–2 Kings draws much from the theology and language of Deuteronomy. According to the New Testament, Christ "redeemed us from

24

the curse of the law by becoming a curse for us" when he hung on the cross (Gal. 3:13).

SACRIFICE² AND FEAST. After the ark is brought into the temple and Solomon prays before the people, Solomon and the people of Israel offer a vast number of sheep and oxen as peace offerings in order to dedicate the temple (8:62–63). They also consecrate the middle portion of the court before the temple by offering "the burnt offering and the grain offering and the fat pieces of the peace offerings" (8:64). Then Solomon and all the people of Israel hold a seven-day feast (8:65), after which they return to their homes "joyful and glad of heart for all the goodness that the LORD had shown to David his servant and to Israel his people" (8:66). As mentioned in the study for Week 2, these various offerings draw from Leviticus 1–7, in which God institutes five major types of offerings for his people, each to serve a different function. (For further exploration of these various sacrifices, see the *ESV Study Bible*, pages 217–225.) Here these offerings serve to consecrate the temple, and the feast functions as an act of celebration of the Lord's goodness to and provision for his people. According to the New Testament, Christ has offered the perfect sacrifice that ends all other sacrifices (Heb. 10:12), and his death opens up the access to God symbolized by the temple (Heb. 10:20).

Personal Implications

Take time to reflect on the implications of 1 Kings 5–10 for your own life today. Make notes below on the personal implications for your walk with the Lord of the (1) *Gospel Glimpses*, (2) *Whole-Bible Connections*, (3) *Theological Soundings*, and (4) this passage as a whole.

1. Gospel Glimpses

2. Whole-Bible Connections

3. Theological Soundings

4. 1 Kings 5:1–10:29

▶ As You Finish This Unit . . .

Take a moment now to ask for the Lord's blessing and help as you continue in this study of 1 Kings. And take a moment also to look back through this unit of study, to reflect on some key things that the Lord may be teaching you.

Definitions

[1] **Exodus** – The departure of the people of Israel from Egypt and their journey to Mount Sinai under Moses' leadership (Exodus 1–19; Numbers 33). The exodus demonstrated God's power and care for his people, who had been enslaved by the Egyptians. The annual festival of Passover commemorates God's final plague upon the Egyptians, resulting in Israel's release from Egypt.

[2] **Sacrifice** – An offering to God, often to signify atonement for, or ask forgiveness of, sin. The law of Moses gave detailed instructions regarding various kinds of sacrifices. By his death on the cross, Jesus gave himself as a sacrifice to atone for the sins of believers (Eph. 5:2; Heb. 10:12). Believers are to offer their bodies as living sacrifices to God (Rom. 12:1).

WEEK 4: DISOBEDIENCE, DIVISION, DECLINE

1 Kings 11:1–16:34

The Place of the Passage

First Kings 11 recounts Solomon's tragic turn toward idolatry, as his many foreign wives lead him to worship other gods. Solomon's disobedience is the first step in the long spiral downward that characterizes 1 and 2 Kings, seen especially in the division of the nation in 1 Kings 12 into the northern kingdom of Israel and the southern kingdom of Judah. Several cycles of evil kings from both kingdoms follow in this section of 1 Kings (chs. 11–16), with the sole exception of Asa in Judah. Along the way, God raises up prophets who call the people to repentance.

The Big Picture

In 1 Kings 11–16, God's people pursue idolatry even as God warns them of the destruction that will inevitably result.

> **Reflection and Discussion**

Read through the complete passage for this study, 1 Kings 11–16. Then review the questions below concerning this section of 1 Kings and write your notes on them. (For further background, see the *ESV Study Bible*, pages 617–632; available online at esv.org.)

1. Solomon Turns from the Lord (1 Kings 11)

In 11:1–8, Solomon's love of foreign women turns his heart away from the Lord toward other gods. Is there anything in chapters 1–10 that makes Solomon's disobedience here in chapter 11 less surprising?

In 11:9–43 the Lord responds to Solomon's disobedience by promising to tear the kingdom away from him after his death and by raising up adversaries within his lifetime. How do you see the Lord's judgment on Solomon mitigated with mercy? Consider especially verses 12–13 and 34–39.

2. The Kingdom Is Divided (1 Kings 12)

In 12:1–24, Rehoboam's foolish choice to listen to the counsel of younger men rather than the counsel of his elder advisers results in the division of the kingdom. As you read this story, where do you see God's sovereignty at work amid human foolishness and sin?

In 12:25–33, Jeroboam institutes idolatry in the northern kingdom of Israel. What parallels do you see between this story and Aaron's leading the people into idolatry in Exodus 32?

3. Prophetic Warning (1 Kings 13–14)

In 13:1–10, a man of God prophesies against the altar at Bethel, a prophecy that will be fulfilled during the reign of Josiah (2 Kings 22–23). How does this episode show that God is still in control, despite the sinful reign of Jeroboam? In what ways can you see both God's mercy and his judgment in this story?

Why do you think the narrative of the disobedience of the man of God (13:11–32) is included in 1 Kings? How do you see this story emphasizing larger themes of the book, such as the binding nature of God's prophetic word?

In 1 Kings 14, the tragic reigns of Jeroboam and Rehoboam come to an end. In what ways do you see the consequences of sin catching up with people in this chapter? How do the events of this chapter cast an ominous cloud over the future of both Israel and Judah?

4. Kings of Israel and Judah (1 Kings 15–16)

In 15:16–24, civil war erupts between Israel and Judah. How are the events of this chapter portrayed as the consequences of the earlier behavior of David and his house versus Jeroboam and his house?

First Kings 15:25–16:34 describes a succession of progressively worse kings in Israel. Nadab's rule is quickly overturned by Baasha, thus ending the house of Jeroboam and fulfilling Ahijah's prophecy in 14:5–11. Baasha's house is soon destroyed as well, fulfilling Jehu's prophecy in 16:1–4 and resulting in the rule of Omri, who does more evil than all who come before him. This sad story culminates in the long rule of Omri's son Ahab, who does even more evil than all of his predecessors, including Omri (16:30, 33). As you read this tragic narrative of decline, what effect does it have on you? Where do you see the destructive consequences of sin?

Read through the following three sections on *Gospel Glimpses, Whole-Bible Connections,* and *Theological Soundings.* Then take time to consider the *Personal Implications* these sections may have for you.

Gospel Glimpses

A LAMP IN JERUSALEM. First Kings 11–16 demonstrates God's unconditional resolve to preserve the Davidic monarchy despite the rebellion of Israel against it. When God promises to tear the kingdom away from Solomon, he makes the concession that he will leave one tribe to Solomon's line "for the sake of David my servant and for the sake of Jerusalem that I have chosen" (11:13). Later he stipulates that he will leave one tribe to Solomon's line "that David my servant may always have a lamp before me in Jerusalem, the city where I have chosen to put my name" (11:36). Through 1 Kings 12–16, and indeed through the entire book, we find God faithfully preserving the Davidic line. For instance, during the reign of Abijam (Solomon's grandson), although the king's heart was not devoted to the Lord, nonetheless "for David's sake the LORD his God gave him a lamp in Jerusalem" (15:4). The imagery of a burning lamp signals God's unconditional faithfulness to his promises despite the frequent disobedience of his people, directing our expectation to Jesus Christ, the Davidic Messiah[1] who rules "on the throne of David and over his kingdom, to establish it and to uphold it with justice and righteousness from this time forth and forevermore" (Isa. 9:7).

Whole-Bible Connections

SIN AS IDOLATRY.[2] The constant sin in 1 and 2 Kings is the sin of idolatry—forsaking the Lord to serve other gods. Solomon turns from the Lord, we are told, because his heart is led astray toward other gods (1 Kings 11:1–8). Jeroboam's institution of false worship in 1 Kings 12:25–33 establishes a pattern the subsequent kings of Israel will continue to follow throughout 1 and 2 Kings (e.g., 1 Kings 15:26, 34; 16:26, 31; etc.). Israel's exile is directly attributed to the idolatry of Jeroboam (2 Kings 17:21–23; see also 1 Kings 13:34; 14:16). In Judah as well, the repeated sin of evil kings is their leading the people into idolatry (e.g., Rehoboam in 14:21–24), while the essential virtue of godly kings is their removal of idolatry (e.g., Asa in 15:11–13). The emphasis on idolatry in 1 and 2 Kings draws upon a larger pattern throughout the Bible that describes sin in terms of idolatry. For instance, the first and second of the Ten Commandments prohibit idolatry (Ex. 20:3–6), and in the New Testament the reception of the gospel is depicted as turning from idols to the true God (1 Thess. 1:9).

Theological Soundings

PROPHETIC WORD. First Kings 11–16 sees a spike in prophetic activity, as "the word of the Lord" comes frequently to God's people (11:29–39; 12:23–24; 13:1–3, 18, 21–22; 14:6–16; 16:1–4). The binding nature of the prophetic word is emphasized in these chapters (e.g., 12:15; 13:32), such that prophets are in authority even over kings (13:4–6), although they themselves are subject to their own prophetic word (13:11–34). The drama of 1 and 2 Kings makes it unmistakably clear that God's word is absolutely sovereign, and whatever it foretells will come to pass. Those who ignore its warnings, such as Jeroboam, do so at their own peril (see 1 Kings 13:33–34).

DIVINE SOVEREIGNTY AND HUMAN RESPONSIBILITY. In 1 Kings 12:1–24, the division of the kingdom is the result of Rehoboam's foolish choice to listen to the counsel of younger men rather than his older and wiser advisers. Nonetheless, Rehoboam's behavior is explained as "a turn of affairs brought about by the LORD that he might fulfill his word, which the LORD spoke by Ahijah the Shilonite to Jeroboam" (12:15). Later, when the people of Judah consider going to war with Israel because of the split in the kingdom, God forbids them from fighting, explaining that "this thing is from me" (12:24). This is a striking instance of the compatibility of human responsibility and divine sovereignty, for even though Rehoboam is responsible for his foolish actions, God is nonetheless sovereignly bringing to pass the fulfillment of his prophetic word through that very behavior.

Personal Implications

Take time to reflect on the implications of 1 Kings 11–16 for your own life today. Make notes below on the personal implications for your walk with the Lord of the (1) *Gospel Glimpses*, (2) *Whole-Bible Connections*, (3) *Theological Soundings*, and (4) this passage as a whole.

1. Gospel Glimpses

2. Whole-Bible Connections

3. Theological Soundings

4. 1 Kings 11:1–16:34

▶ As You Finish This Unit . . .

Take a moment now to ask for the Lord's blessing and help as you continue in this study of 1 Kings. And take a moment also to look back through this unit of study, to reflect on some key things that the Lord may be teaching you.

Definitions

[1] **Messiah** – Transliteration of a Hebrew word meaning "anointed one," the equivalent of the Greek word *Christ*. This term was originally applied to anyone specially designated for a particular role, such as a king or a priest. Jesus himself affirmed that he was the royal Messiah sent from God (Matt. 16:16–17).

[2] **Idolatry** – In the Bible, this term usually refers to the worship of a physical object identified with a cosmic power. Paul's comments in Colossians 3:5, however, suggest that idolatry includes covetousness, which is essentially equivalent to worshiping material things.

WEEK 5: ELIJAH AND COVENANT RENEWAL

1 Kings 17:1–19:21

▲

Chapters 17–19 represent a slowing down of the narrative pace of 1 Kings, as God raises up the prophet Elijah to confront the Baal[1] worship introduced to Israel by Ahab and his foreign wife, Jezebel. In chapter 17, God sustains Elijah through drought, first through ravens at the Cherith brook and then through a widow in Zarephath. Chapter 18 narrates a dramatic showdown between Elijah and the prophets of Baal, as the Lord reveals that he is the true God and brings the drought to an end. In chapter 19 a disillusioned Elijah flees from Jezebel, and his successor, Elisha, is announced.

The Big Picture

First Kings 17–19 shows that the God of Israel, not Baal, is the true God, and that he accomplishes his purposes amid the changing seasons of life.

> **Reflection and Discussion**

Read through the complete passage for this study, 1 Kings 17–19. Then review the questions below concerning this introductory section of 1 Kings and write your notes on them. (For further background, see the *ESV Study Bible*, pages 632–637; available online at esv.org.)

1. Elijah during the Drought (1 Kings 17)

In Canaanite religion, Baal was thought to be the god of storms, holding particular power over rain and fertility. In light of this, why do you think God sent judgment in the specific form of a drought? What message would this have sent?

Throughout this chapter, Elijah holds incredible power as God's prophet, commanding the rain at his own word (17:1). And yet this is a difficult, lonely, and humbling season as well. He must live alone in the wilderness before traveling north to Zarephath to live on the outskirts of society with a Gentile widow and her son. Food was scarce in both places. What do you think would have been most difficult about this experience for Elijah? How do you think this season would have required him to trust in the Lord while preparing him for what was ahead?

In what ways do you see God's provision for Elijah in this chapter? In light of 18:10, could the very obscurity of Elijah's circumstances be one expression of

God's provision and care for him? Are there any lessons we can draw from this chapter about how God is at work during the "wilderness seasons" of life?

What is the widow's response when Elijah raises her son from the grave (17:24)? What light might this shed on the purpose of this episode in relation to the larger context of the struggle between Baal and the God of Israel throughout these chapters?

2. The Contest on Mount Carmel (1 Kings 18)

What does Elijah's conversation with Obadiah in 18:1–16 reveal about the state of affairs in Israel after the drought, and about Elijah's reputation in particular?

The contest on Mount Carmel in 18:20–40 demonstrates unmistakably that the Lord, not Baal, is the true and living God. How do the details of the story reinforce this message? Consider, for instance, Elijah's taunting (18:27), the extremes to which the prophets of Baal go (18:28–29), and the extra water poured on Elijah's altar (18:33–40).

3. Elijah at Horeb (1 Kings 19)

In 19:1–8, a despairing Elijah flees at the threat of Jezebel, asking the Lord to take his life, "for I am no better than my fathers" (19:4). Throughout 1 and 2 Kings, prophets and their disciples are often depicted using father/son language (1 Kings 13:11–12; 2 Kings 2:12; 6:21). In light of this, what do you think is prompting Elijah's seemingly bizarre turn of emotions in this story? What larger message may Jezebel's threat have represented?

At Horeb, God appears to Elijah through various natural phenomena (a wind, an earthquake, and a fire), but each time the text repeats, "The Lord was not in [it]." Then God sends a "low whisper," and the refrain is not repeated. What do you think God is seeking to communicate to Elijah at this point? Based on the fact that Elijah responds in identical language before and after this episode (see 19:10, 14), do you think he got the message?

Throughout 1 Kings 18–19, Elijah expresses the belief that he is the only true prophet left in Israel (18:22; 19:10, 14). However, God declares that he has preserved a remnant of seven thousand of his people (19:18). What do you think caused Elijah to overlook all of these others who were loyal to the Lord? How do you think Christians can fall into a similar mind-set concerning the church today?

Read through the following three sections on *Gospel Glimpses*, *Whole-Bible Connections*, and *Theological Soundings*. Then take time to consider the *Personal Implications* these sections may have for you.

Gospel Glimpses

DEATH AND RESURRECTION. The great message of 1 Kings 17–19 is that God, not Baal, is the true God, a message particularly emphasized in Elijah's raising of the widow's son (17:17–24). In Canaanite thought, Baal was believed to periodically die, submitting to the god of death, Mot, before coming back to life during the rainy season. The resurrection of the widow's son reinforces that it is the God of Israel, not Baal, who holds power over the grave—just as the drought reveals that it is the God of Israel who controls the weather. God's power over the grave would be more fully manifested later in redemptive history through the person of Christ, who would conquer death forever by submitting to it himself before rising again.

Whole-Bible Connections

PASSING BY AT HOREB. Horeb is another name for Sinai, the mountain on which God manifested himself to Moses and the people of Israel and gave them his law. On this mountain, God descended to Moses in a cloud, passing before Moses and revealing his glory while Moses hid in a cleft of the rock (Ex. 33:17–34:9). Like Moses, Elijah stands in a cave on this mountain as God passes by in his glory (1 Kings 19:11–12). Elijah's journey of 40 days and 40 nights (19:8) may also recall Moses' 40 days and 40 nights on Sinai (Ex. 24:18). In the New Testament, on another mountain, a cloud of glory passes over Jesus Christ, who is accompanied by these very two men, Moses and Elijah—whom many see as representing the Law and the Prophets, respectively (Mark 9:2–13). This incident in 1 Kings 19 is therefore not only an important moment in Elijah's ministry and the struggle against Baal worship but is also one of several instances of theophany[2] in the Bible that find their ultimate trajectory and fulfillment in the ministry of Christ.

THE LORD ALONE IS GOD. All throughout Israel's history, God calls his people to exclusive, unrivaled commitment and worship (e.g., Deut. 6:4–5). The people of Israel, from the golden calf of Aaron (Exodus 32) to the golden calves of Jeroboam (1 Kings 12:25–33), frequently turn aside from this calling to worship God alone, as they worship other gods instead. Perhaps in no other place in the Bible is God's exclusive claim to deity more evident, or the choice between the true God and idols more poignant, than in 1 Kings 18. As the prophets of Baal cry out for an answer during the contest at Carmel, we read that "there was no voice, and no one answered" (1 Kings 18:26); "no one answered; no one paid attention" (v. 29). The story emphasizes the absolute powerlessness of idols and the Lord's exclusive power to save. This theme will be picked up again and again in the prophets (e.g., Hab. 2:18–20), and in the New Testament Paul will declare, "We know that 'an idol has no real existence,' and that 'there is no God but one'" (1 Cor. 8:4).

Theological Soundings

GOD'S FAITHFULNESS. God is faithful to Elijah throughout these chapters, as seen in his providing for Elijah's needs during drought, protecting him from Ahab's spies, answering his prayer for fire from heaven, and gently confronting him in his disillusionment and self-pity. He is faithful to his people as well: judging evil, preserving a remnant,[3] and fulfilling his promises. When Elijah laments that he is the only true prophet left, for instance, God announces his plans to stamp out further rebellion through Jehu and Elisha (19:17). These chapters evidence God's resourcefulness in bringing about his purposes. Although Elijah cannot see it, God is in the gentle whisper of chapter 19 as well as in the fire from heaven of chapter 18—and he is just as able to carry forward his plan through preserving a remnant as through national revival.

Personal Implications

Take time to reflect on the implications of 1 Kings 17–19 for your own life today. Make notes below on the personal implications for your walk with the Lord of the (1) *Gospel Glimpses*, (2) *Whole-Bible Connections*, (3) *Theological Soundings*, and (4) this passage as a whole.

1. Gospel Glimpses

2. Whole-Bible Connections

3. Theological Soundings

4. 1 Kings 17:1–19:21

As You Finish This Unit . . .

Take a moment now to ask for the Lord's blessing and help as you continue in this study of 1 Kings. And take a moment also to look back through this unit of study, to reflect on some key things that the Lord may be teaching you.

Definitions

[1] **Baal** – An ancient Semitic deity associated with storms, holding particular power, it was thought, over rain and fertility. Baal worship was a strong temptation to Israel during most of her history.

[2] **Theophany** – A manifestation of God's presence to people, often accompanied by physical phenomena such as clouds or fire.

[3] **Remnant** – In the Bible, a portion of faithful people who remain after most others are destroyed by some catastrophe. The notion of a "remnant" can be found in various events recorded in Scripture, including the flood (Genesis 6–8) and Judah's return from exile (Ezra 8).

Week 6: Ahab's Death and Elijah's Departure

1 Kings 20:1–2 Kings 2:25

First Kings 20–22 describes the further reign of Ahab after his confrontation with Elijah. Although the full destruction of Ahab's house is delayed when he humbles himself before God (21:27–29), Ahab's own death, foretold by multiple prophets, is inevitable (22:29–40). Elijah returns to the scene in 2 Kings 1 to confront Ahab's son Ahaziah, and the prophet is then succeeded by Elisha in 2 Kings 2. At that point the events foretold in 1 Kings 19:15–17, which will bring to conclusion the long struggle against Baal worship, can come to pass.

The Big Picture

In 1 Kings 20–2 Kings 2 we see God patiently bringing about his purposes for his people in judgment and salvation. These "bridge chapters" between 1–2 Kings also demonstrate the binding nature of prophetic oracles.

> ### Reflection and Discussion

Read through the complete passage for this study, 1 Kings 20–2 Kings 2. Then review the questions below concerning this section of 1 and 2 Kings and write your notes on them. (For further background, see the *ESV Study Bible*, pages 637–649; available online at esv.org.)

1. Ahab's Wars with Syria (1 Kings 20)

Ahab is engaged in two military conflicts with Ben-hadad of Syria in 20:1–34. Why do you think God instructs Ahab to allow the governors' servants to initiate the fighting in verse 14? How does the result of these conflicts undermine the Assyrians' mistaken beliefs about the God of Israel (see v. 28)?

How does the seemingly strange behavior of the prophet in 20:35–37 emphasize the binding nature of his pronouncement in verse 42? Do you see any parallels between this episode and the similar one recounted in 13:11–34?

2. Naboth's Vineyard (1 Kings 21)

In 21:1–16, Ahab and Jezebel conspire against Naboth to seize his vineyard. What does this episode reveal about the character of Ahab? Of Jezebel?

In what ways is Elijah's pronouncement in 21:17–29 a just response to Ahab's treachery? What do these verses teach us about the relation between God's justice and his mercy?

3. Micaiah's Prophecy and Ahab's Death (1 Kings 22)

How do (good) Jehoshaphat and (evil) Ahab respond differently to the prospect of battle and Micaiah's prophecy throughout 22:1–28? What does the treatment of Micaiah as the sole prophet of the Lord reveal about the spiritual state of Ahab, and of Israel under Ahab's reign?

How do the details of Ahab's death in 22:29–40 reflect God's sovereignty and his commitment to fulfill the word given to Micaiah?

4. Elijah Confronts Ahaziah (2 Kings 1)

In 2 Kings 1 Ahaziah inquires of Baal-zebub, the god of Ekron, concerning his illness. Elijah confronts Ahaziah for failing to inquire of the Lord, and when the king attempts to compel Elijah's presence, the prophet repeatedly calls down fire on the king's soldiers. What message do you think readers are supposed to draw from this story? What does it reveal about God's power and character?

5. Elisha Succeeds Elijah (2 Kings 2)

How do various details related in 2 Kings 2 reinforce the message that the mantle of Elijah's leadership and spiritual authority has been passed to Elisha? How do others react to them both? What are their common behaviors? What is the significance of Elisha's initial activity following Elijah's departure?

To modern readers, the judgments of fire from heaven (2 Kings 1:9–12) and mauling by bears (2:23–25) can seem harsh. But throughout 1 and 2 Kings, how people treat the Lord's prophets often reflects their deeper attitude toward the Lord himself. How might this insight help us understand the appropriateness of these events?

Read through the following three sections on *Gospel Glimpses*, *Whole-Bible Connections*, and *Theological Soundings*. Then take time to consider the *Personal Implications* these sections may have for you.

▶ Gospel Glimpses

JUDGMENT[1] AND MERCY.[2] A recurring theme throughout these chapters is God's unwavering commitment to establish justice and to punish evil. On several occasions the equitable nature of justice is emphasized. Thus one prophet informs Ahab, "Your life shall be for his life" (1 Kings 20:42); another promises, "In the place where dogs licked up the blood of Naboth shall dogs lick your own blood" (21:19). At the same time, even wicked Ahab can receive mercy when he humbles himself before the Lord (21:27–29). The cross of Jesus Christ represents the ultimate expression of both God's judgment and his mercy, for at the cross God took the judgment of his people onto himself in the person of Christ. It was "his life for our life," fulfilling God's commitment to justice while allowing for his free and inexhaustible expression of mercy toward all who humble themselves before it.

▶ Whole-Bible Connections

CROSSING OVER PARTED WATERS. In 2 Kings 2:8, Elijah strikes the Jordan River with his rolled-up cloak; the water parts, and he and Elisha pass over on dry ground. Elisha crosses back over by himself in the same way after Elijah's departure to heaven (2:14). This event recalls not only Moses' parting of the Red Sea in Exodus 14 but also Joshua's parting of the Jordan River in Joshua 3. The recapitulation of these miracles signals the transfer of authority from one leader to the next: as Joshua inherited the spiritual authority of Moses, so Elisha has inherited the prophetic mantle of Elijah.

THE BATTLE BELONGS TO THE LORD. Throughout these chapters, God's work often confounds human wisdom and surpasses human strength. Battles are won through inexperienced servants leading the way (1 Kings 20:14); truth is revealed to Micaiah alone, while hundreds of other prophets are deceived by a lying spirit (1 Kings 22:13–28); multiple squads of 50 soldiers are not enough to secure the capture of Elijah (2 Kings 1:9–15). These events fit with a pattern throughout the Bible in which God often works through the weak, the ordinary, the outsider, in ways contrary to human wisdom and offensive to human expectation. One thinks of tiny David slaying the giant Goliath (1 Sam. 17:49), God reducing the size of Gideon's army (Judges 7), or Paul's assertion that God chose the weak to shame the strong (1 Cor. 1:27–28). In the language of Proverbs 21:31, "The horse is made ready for the day of battle, but the victory belongs to the LORD."

Theological Soundings

THE PROPHETIC WORD. Prophetic activity spikes once again in this "bridge" between 1 and 2 Kings (1 Kings 20:13–14, 22, 28, 41–43; 21:17–24; 22:13–28; 2 Kings 1:3–4, 15–16; 2:21–22) as various events are declared in advance by one of God's prophets. The emphasis falls on the binding nature of prophetic oracles: whatever the prophets foretell must come to pass, and even the prophets themselves are subject to it (1 Kings 20:35–36; compare 1 Kings 13:11–34). The narratives recorded in this portion of the Bible evidence the truth of Lamentations 3:37 ("Who has spoken and it came to pass, unless the Lord has commanded it?") and Isaiah 46:11 ("I have spoken, and I will bring it to pass; I have purposed, and I will do it").

HEAVEN.[3] References to heaven are relatively rare in the Old Testament, especially in its earlier portions. It is more common to find references to "going down" to Sheol, although it is wrong to assume that the ancient Israelites had no conception of living in God's presence after death. The hope of an afterlife in the presence of God is expressed, for instance, in Enoch's departure in Genesis 5:24, as well as in Psalms 16:10–11 and 49:14–15. Elijah's departure to heaven in 2 Kings 2:11–12 makes an important contribution to the biblical conception of heaven. The chariots and horses of fire may be a reference to heavenly angelic armies; they will reappear in 2 Kings 6:17 (and possibly 7:6). That Elijah is taken up bodily to heaven in a whirlwind makes it clear that, contrary to much other ancient thought, heaven is a real place that physical creatures can enter. In Acts 1:9–11 the risen Christ also ascends bodily into heaven.

Personal Implications

Take time to reflect on the implications of 1 Kings 20–2 Kings 2 for your own life today. Make notes below on the personal implications for your walk with the Lord of the (1) *Gospel Glimpses*, (2) *Whole-Bible Connections*, (3) *Theological Soundings*, and (4) this passage as a whole.

1. Gospel Glimpses

2. Whole-Bible Connections

3. Theological Soundings

4. 1 Kings 20:1–2 Kings 2:25

▶ As You Finish This Unit . . .

Take a moment now to ask for the Lord's blessing and help as you continue in this study of 1 Kings. And take a moment also to look back through this unit of study, to reflect on some key things that the Lord may be teaching you.

Definitions

[1] **Judgment** – Any assessment of something or someone, especially moral assessment. The Bible also speaks of a final day of judgment when Christ returns, when all those who have refused to repent will be judged (Rev. 20:12–15).

[2] **Mercy** – Compassion and kindness toward someone experiencing hardship, sometimes even when such suffering results from the person's own sin or foolishness. God displays mercy toward his people and they, in turn, are called to display mercy toward others (Luke 6:36).

[3] **Heaven** – The sky, or the abode of God (Matt. 6:9), which is commonly regarded as being above the earth and sky. As the abode of God, heaven is also the place where believers live in God's presence after death (1 Thess. 4:16–17).

Week 7: Elisha and the Prophetic Word

2 Kings 3:1–8:6

▲

This large section of 2 Kings focuses on the ministry of Elisha the prophet. Just before Elijah's departure, Elisha had asked him for a double portion of his spirit, and the many miracles[1] he performs in this section show that his request has been answered. Elisha's ministry testifies to God's faithfulness and commitment to his people even when they continue to drift from him.

The Big Picture

God accomplishes his purposes for both judgment and salvation among wayward Israel through the miracles and prophetic word of Elisha the prophet.

Reflection and Discussion

Read through the complete passage for this study, 2 Kings 3:1–8:6. Then review the questions below concerning this section of 2 Kings and write your notes on them. (For further background, see the *ESV Study Bible*, pages 649–658; available online at esv.org.)

1. War with Moab (2 Kings 3)

Unlike during a previous battle with Syria in 1 Kings 22 (see especially 22:5), in this conflict Jehoshaphat inquires of the Lord only after difficulty has emerged. In what ways do you see this military effort receiving God's favor, and in what ways do you see it lacking God's favor?

2. Miracles of Elisha (2 Kings 4)

Second Kings 4 records various miracles performed by Elisha, including a miraculous supply of oil for the widow of one of the prophets (4:1–7), the conception and later the resuscitation of a Shunammite's son (4:8–37), and provision of food for the company of prophets (4:38–44). In what ways do the details of these miracles mirror the earlier miracles of Elijah, in line with the prophetic succession depicted in 2:9? What future miracles do they prefigure?

How do the specific miracles Elisha performs demonstrate God's care for his people and his responsiveness to them?

3. Naaman Is Cured of Leprosy (2 Kings 5)

Why do you think Naaman becomes angry at Elisha's instructions (v. 12)? Given Naaman's status as commander of the army, how do you think this encounter was different from the way in which he was usually treated?

How does Naaman's response to his healing fulfill Solomon's petitions in 1 Kings 8:41–43 for Gentiles to know the true God through the nation of Israel? Consider especially Naaman's declaration and confession in 2 Kings 5:15–18.

In 5:20–27, Gehazi uses Elisha's miracle for monetary profit, and is accordingly punished for his greed. According to Gehazi's words in verse 20, and Elisha's in verse 27, how would you characterize the motivation behind his behavior?

4. Conflict with Syria (2 Kings 6–7)

In 6:8–23, God protects Elisha from an army of Syrian horses and chariots. What do the details of this story reveal about God's gracious character and his protection of his people? What contemporary application might Elisha's statement in verse 16 ("Those who are with us are more than those who are with them") have for Christians experiencing persecution today?

In 6:24–7:20, the Syrians' siege of Samaria under Ben-hadad results in a terrible famine. How is the truthfulness of Elisha's word proven through the events of this story (see especially vv. 17–20)? What conclusion about "the word of the Lord" do you think the reader is intended to draw from this story?

5. The Shunammite Woman (2 Kings 8:1–6)

Why do you think God included this story of the Shunammite woman within the larger narrative of 1 and 2 Kings? What does this story reveal about God's care for outsiders?

Read through the following three sections on *Gospel Glimpses*, *Whole-Bible Connections*, and *Theological Soundings*. Then take time to consider the *Personal Implications* these sections may have for you.

Gospel Glimpses

GOD'S CARE FOR HIS PEOPLE. The various miracles recounted in these chapters (2 Kings 3–8) reflect God's gracious care for his people and his responsiveness to their expressions of faith. God's mercy extends particularly to the marginalized, the outsider, the forgotten—the widow from among the company of the prophets (4:1–7), for instance, or the four lepers outside the city gate of Samaria (7:3–15). Even the recovery of a borrowed axe head among the sons of the prophets is not too unimportant for God to notice (6:1–7). Of particular significance is God's mercy to non-Israelites, who stand outside of covenant relationship with him—large sections of these chapters are devoted to God's care for the Syrian army commander Naaman (5:1–19), and also for the Shunammite woman (4:18–37; 8:1–6). God's gracious care for all the peoples of the earth finds its fullest expression in the work of Christ, through whom Gentiles who come to faith in Christ are fully embraced as the people of God and inherit all of his promises (2 Cor. 1:20–22; Gal. 3:7).

Whole-Bible Connections

GREED AND JUDGMENT. Gehazi's greed in 5:15–27 reflects a tragically common pattern in the Bible of foolish attempts to use God's miraculous work to gain wealth. "The love of money is a root of all kinds of evils," the apostle Paul warns (1 Tim. 6:10). In Joshua 7, Achan sins by stealing treasure devoted to destruction, bringing guilt and judgment on all Israel. The early church was also tempted by greed and the misuse of spiritual power, such as in Ananias and Saphira's dishonesty (Acts 5:1–11) or Simon the magician's attempted bribery (Acts 8:18–24). Most infamously, Judas Iscariot betrayed Christ, the precious Son of God, for a mere 30 pieces of silver (Matt. 26:14–15).

SPIRITUAL SUCCESSION. Many of the miracles of Elisha seem to mirror those of Elijah. As Elijah raises from the dead a Gentile woman's son (1 Kings 17:17–24), so does Elisha (2 Kings 4:18–37); if Elijah can call down fire from heaven (1 Kings 18:36–40), so can Elisha (2 Kings 1:9–12); even little details like miraculous provision through a jar of oil attend both of their ministries (1 Kings 17:8–16; 2 Kings 4:1–7). These similarities seem to demonstrate the fulfillment of Elisha's request for a double portion of Elijah's spirit (2 Kings 2:9–11) and reflect a common pattern throughout Scripture in which spiritual authority and leadership are transferred from one individual to another. The book of Joshua, for instance, seems to depict a similar Moses–Joshua succession (Josh. 1:1–9; compare Deut. 31:1–8; 34:9), and in the book of Acts, many of Paul's miracles seem to mirror earlier miracles of Peter (e.g., Acts 5:15; 19:11–12), expressing the extension and continuation of God's work.

Theological Soundings

MIRACLES. Many kinds of miracles are seen throughout these chapters (2 Kings 3–8), typically performed by Elisha the prophet. As depicted in this portion of Scripture, miracles are a manifestation of God's sovereign power (3:16–20), demonstrating the trustworthiness of his word and character (4:17, 44; 7:18–20). Miracles are often in response to the needs of God's people (see 4:1–7, 38–44), while also serving to advance God's purposes among those outside the nation of Israel (4:18–37; 5:1–19; 8:1–6). While miracles can strengthen the faith of those who benefit from them (5:15–19a), they often offend human expectation and pride (5:11–12; 7:1–2) and are no guarantee of spiritual fruit in the lives of those who benefit from them (5:15–27).

ANGELS. [2] Twice in military conflict with Syria, God's people are rescued by horses and chariots of fire (6:17; 7:6 [implied]). Earlier, when Elijah was taken to heaven, he was separated from Elisha by these same chariots and horses of fire, whom Elisha called "the chariots of Israel and its horsemen" (2:12). This seems to refer to God's divine (angelic) army—elsewhere in the Old Testament, angels are depicted using similar horse/chariot imagery (e.g., Zech. 1:7–17), and fire is often associated with God's presence throughout Scripture. Although angels are not typically visible to human eyes (Elisha has to pray for his servant to see them; 2 Kings 6:17), they nonetheless interact with this world and work toward God's purposes (e.g., Heb. 1:14; 13:2).

Personal Implications

Take time to reflect on the implications of 2 Kings 3:1–8:6 for your own life today. Make notes below on the personal implications for your walk with the Lord of the (1) *Gospel Glimpses*, (2) *Whole-Bible Connections*, (3) *Theological Soundings*, and (4) this passage as a whole.

1. Gospel Glimpses

2. Whole-Bible Connections

3. Theological Soundings

4. 2 Kings 3:1–8:6

As You Finish This Unit . . .

Take a moment now to ask for the Lord's blessing and help as you continue in this study of 2 Kings. And take a moment also to look back through this unit of study, to reflect on some key things that the Lord may be teaching you.

Definitions

[1] **Miracle** – A special act of God that goes beyond natural means, thus demonstrating God's power.

[2] **Angel** – A supernatural messenger of God, often sent to carry out his will or to assist human beings in carrying out his will. Although angels are more powerful than humans and often instill awe, they are not to be worshiped (Col. 2:18; Rev. 22:8–9). The Bible does, however, note various appearances of an "angel of the Lord," apparently a physical manifestation of God himself.

WEEK 8:
JEHU AND JEHOASH:
JUDGMENT AND REFORM

2 Kings 8:7–12:21

After an extended focus on Elisha's miraculous ministry, the predictions of 1 Kings 19:15–18 are now fulfilled, beginning with Hazael's murder of Ben-hadad (2 Kings 8:7–15) and followed by the destruction of the house of Ahab by Jehu (chs. 9–10). Jehu also kills Ahaziah king of Judah, and God therefore raises up a new Judean king, Jehoash (also called Joash), who halts the spiritual decline of Judah by bringing reform to temple worship (chs. 11–12).

The Big Picture

God fulfills his promises to judge evil while raising up those who will bring reformation and renewal to his people.

> ### Reflection and Discussion

Read through the complete passage for this study, 2 Kings 8:7–12:21. Then review the questions below concerning this section of 2 Kings and write your notes on them. (For further background, see the *ESV Study Bible*, pages 658–668; available online at esv.org.)

1. Hazael, Jehoram, and Ahaziah (2 Kings 8:7–29)

How does Hazael's murder of Ben-hadad in 8:7–15 fulfill the earlier predictions of Elijah? How do you see this episode fitting in with the larger struggle against Baal worship?

The reigns of two evil kings of Judah, Jehoram and Ahaziah, are recorded in 8:16–29. What clues do you see in this section that the southern kingdom of Judah has become dangerously interconnected with the northern kingdom of Israel— particularly the houses of Ahab and Omri? Consider especially verses 18 and 26.

2. Judgment from Jehu (2 Kings 9–10)

In 9:1–13, one of the prophets under Elisha's leadership anoints Jehu as king of Israel. How does this prophet's oracle against the house of Ahab in verses 6–10 differ from the oracle in 1 Kings 21:21–24? How is it similar?

God's reason for anointing Jehu in 2 Kings 9:6–10 is to execute judgment on the house of Ahab, in line with the earlier predictions of Elijah (1 Kings 19:15–18; 21:21–24, 29). Here, and many other times in 1–2 Kings, God's promises take longer to come about than we might expect. Why do you think God's judgments against evil are sometimes delayed? What relevance might this have for our lives today?

In 2 Kings 9:25–26, Jehu throws the dead body of Joram onto the plot of ground that had belonged to Naboth. The words "I will repay you" in the Lord's pronouncement of verse 26 show that Jehu's actions are ultimately an expression of the Lord's judgment, in fulfillment of Elijah's prophecy against the house of Ahab in 1 Kings 21. That God can accomplish his purposes through such bloody means can be difficult for many modern readers to understand. But what does this passage reveal about God's passion for justice, and his concern for Naboth? What contribution do these events make to the biblical portrait of God's character?

What is the significance of Jezebel's being trampled on and eaten by dogs in 2 Kings 9:36–37, rather than being buried?

61

In 2 Kings 10, Jehu continues his purge of the houses of Ahab (vv. 1–11, 15–17) and Ahaziah (vv. 12–14) while also bringing Baal worship to an end (vv. 18–28). Nonetheless, despite these accomplishments for which he is commended, Jehu continues to walk in the sin of Jeroboam (vv. 29–31), and Israel loses territory during his reign (vv. 32–36). Looking at Jehu's reign as a whole, and considering God's evaluation of him in 10:28–31, would you consider Jehu more of a "good" king or a "bad" king? Why?

3. The Reign of Jehoash (2 Kings 10–11)

In chapter 11, a new threat arises in Judah after Ahaziah's death, as Athaliah begins killing off the royal family. After her reign is overthrown by the high priest Jehoiada, the people renew their covenant with the Lord and with King Jehoash (11:17–19), resulting in joy and peace in the land (11:20). Temple reform will come in the next chapter, but what concern do you already see for the purity of temple precincts in the details of this chapter?

How do the efforts at repairing the temple get delayed in chapter 12? What measures does Jehoiada take to set the work back on track?

In what ways is the repair of the temple under the leadership of Jehoash and Jehoiada, though noble, ultimately disappointing? See especially verses 13, 17–18.

Read through the following three sections on *Gospel Glimpses*, *Whole-Bible Connections*, and *Theological Soundings*. Then take time to consider the *Personal Implications* these sections may have for you.

Gospel Glimpses

DIVINE JUDGMENT. A theme throughout these chapters is God's judgment against evil. This portion of Scripture emphasizes God's passionate commitment to justice and his unswerving faithfulness in bringing wrongdoing to account—not only in the case of the false prophets of Baal (10:18–27) and oppressive foreign rulers like Ben-hadad (8:7–15), but also in the case of wicked rulers among the people of God, such as Joram (9:14–26), Ahaziah (9:27–28), Jezebel (9:30–37), and Athaliah (11:4–16). These chapters remind us that God avenges the blood of his servants (9:7), he sees and repays evil (9:26), and his judgment is inescapable (10:10). The cross of Jesus Christ is the ultimate expression of divine judgment: Jesus triumphed over the author of evil, Satan himself (Col. 2:14–15), and bore God's judgment in the place of his people, so that they no longer live under divine judgment but enjoy divine favor and mercy (Rom. 5:1; 8:1).

Whole-Bible Connections

THE DAVIDIC LAMP. In describing the evil reign of Jehoram of Judah, the author declares that "The LORD was not willing to destroy Judah, for the sake of David his servant, since he promised to give a lamp to him and to his sons forever" (2 Kings 8:19; see also 1 Kings 11:36; 15:4). This verse reminds us of the distinction in God's purposes for Judah and for Israel,[1] which had been blurred somewhat through intermarriage as the infidelity of the house of Ahab bled into the lineage of Judah (see 2 Kings 8:18, 27). (Later, Jehu must slay not only Joram of Israel but also Ahaziah of Judah to cleanse the nation from evil.) Yet while God will bring other dynasties to complete destruction, he will only *chastise* the house of David, because of his promise to provide a lamp to the sons of David forever. The promise for an everlasting Davidic rule is realized ultimately in the coming and reign of Christ (Luke 1:32–33). (See also the discussion of "A Lamp in Jerusalem" in Week 4, "Gospel Glimpses.")

COVENANT RENEWAL. After Athaliah is put to death in 2 Kings 11, Jehoiada, the chief priest, leads the people in a renewal of their covenant with the Lord and with the king (11:17–20). This reflects a pattern throughout Scripture in which the people of God during times of spiritual revival reaffirm their covenant commitments before the Lord (e.g., under Joshua in Joshua 24; Josiah in 2 Kings 23; Nehemiah in Nehemiah 8–10). In the New Testament, we remember and receive the benefits of the new covenant afresh each time we partake of the Lord's Supper (Luke 22:19–20).

Theological Soundings

WORSHIP REFORM. Amid the Baal worship that had occupied God's people during the preceding years, the temple had fallen into neglect. Second Kings 8–12 emphasizes the purity of the temple and the importance of temple worship in the life of God's people. Jehoash's coronation ceremony takes place within the temple courts (2 Kings 11:11–12), while the slaughtering of wicked Athaliah must not occur within the temple confines (v. 15). When Jehoash begins to rule after a long period of Baal worship, repair of the temple is desperately needed (12:4–16). This portion of Scripture emphasizes the importance of the worship of God's people as they draw near to God in accordance with the institutions he has ordained.

THE INESCAPABILITY OF GOD'S WORD. These chapters join earlier portions of 1–2 Kings in emphasizing the binding, inescapable nature of God's Word—particularly with respect to earlier oracles of judgment. After judgment is executed, the text frequently records that "This was done to fulfill the word of the Lord spoken by . . ." This is the case with respect to the judgment of Joram (9:25–26), Jezebel (9:36–37), the house of Ahab in Jezreel (10:10), and the house of Ahab in Samaria (10:17). As Jehu puts it in 10:10, "There shall fall to the earth nothing of the word of the LORD, which the LORD spoke concerning the house of Ahab, for the LORD has done what he said by his servant Elijah." These events would have been all the more meaningful because of the passage of time between the prophetic word and its fulfillment. This portion of Scripture reminds us that when God pronounces judgment, even though it may be delayed for a while, it will certainly come to pass.

Personal Implications

Take time to reflect on the implications of 2 Kings 8:7–12:21 for your own life today. Make notes below on the personal implications for your walk with the Lord of the (1) *Gospel Glimpses*, (2) *Whole-Bible Connections*, (3) *Theological Soundings*, and (4) this passage as a whole.

1. Gospel Glimpses

2. Whole-Bible Connections

3. Theological Soundings

4. 2 Kings 8:7–12:21

As You Finish This Unit . . .

Take a moment now to ask for the Lord's blessing and help as you continue in this study of 2 Kings. And take a moment also to look back through this unit of study, to reflect on some key things that the Lord may be teaching you.

Definitions

[1] **Israel** – Originally, another name given to Jacob (Gen. 32:28). The name is later applied to the nation formed by his descendants, then to the 10 northern tribes of that nation, who rejected the anointed king and formed their own nation. In the NT, the name is applied to the church as the spiritual descendants of Abraham (Gal. 6:16).

[2] **Revival** – A renewed desire for spiritual things, brought about by the work of God.

WEEK 9: THE DECLINE AND FALL OF THE NORTHERN KINGDOM

2 Kings 13:1–17:41

The Place of the Passage

Second Kings 13–17 passes relatively quickly through the accessions of numerous kings of both Israel and Judah. The narrative begins by filling in the reigns of the two Israelite kings (Jehoahaz and Jehoash) who ruled during the reign of Jehoash in Judah; it is at this time that Elisha dies as well. Following this, the narrative switches back and forth between Israel and Judah, describing a period of civil war, numerous evil kings in Israel, and several good but ineffective kings in Judah. This period of history is marked by further decline into sin and idolatry among God's people, ending ultimately in the exile of Israel by the Assyrian army.

The Big Picture

God brings judgment upon his people because they have sinned against him by continually pursuing idols.

Reflection and Discussion

Read through the complete passage for this study, 2 Kings 13–17. Then review the questions below concerning this section of 2 Kings and write your notes on them. (For further background, see the *ESV Study Bible*, pages 668–680; available online at esv.org.)

1. Jehoahaz, Jehoash, and the Death of Elisha (2 Kings 13)

How would you characterize the spiritual state of Israel under the reign of Jehoahaz (13:1–9)? In what ways does this time in Israel's history reflect that of the book of Judges?

Why is Elisha angry with Jehoash for striking the ground only three times (13:14–19)? What do Jehoash's actions indicate about his attitude?

2. Amaziah, Jeroboam II, and Azariah (2 Kings 14:1–15:7)

Israel and Judah fall into conflict and civil war in chapter 14, as Amaziah of Judah confronts Jehoash of Israel and refuses to listen to his taunt (vv. 8–10). What does this conflict reveal about the spiritual state of God's people at this time? What is the result of this conflict (consider especially v. 14)?

What explanation is given for God's compassion toward Israel during the reign of Jeroboam II (14:26–27)? What biblical promise is being referenced here?

3. The Final Kings of Israel (2 Kings 15:8–31)

Israel's kings during the nation's final days are now recounted in rapid succession. In what ways are the events of this section anticipated earlier in 1 and 2 Kings (consider, e.g., 1 Kings 14:15; 2 Kings 10:30; 15:12)?

During the reigns of Zechariah, Shallum, Menahem, Pekahiah, and Pekah, Israel's history is marked by numerous conspiracies against the reigning king, as well as the diminishing status of the region, as the Assyrian empire annexes much of Israel's northern and eastern territory (e.g., 15:29). What other indications of Israel's demise do you see in the text? What overall impression does this portion of 2 Kings give you?

4. Jotham and Ahaz (15:32–16:20)

The reign of Ahaz brings further spiritual corruption to Judah. He practices child sacrifice (16:3–4), accepts vassal status to Assyria (vv. 7–9), and introduces foreign worship into the temple in Jerusalem (vv. 10–18). What do you think motivated Ahaz to copy the altar he saw in Damascus (vv. 10–16)?

_____

_____

_____

_____

_____

_____

5. The Exile of Israel (2 Kings 17:1–41)

In 2 Kings 17:7–23 we find a relatively rare and extended break in the narrative as the author pauses to *interpret* the exile of the northern kingdom that has just been described in 17:1–6. What was the fundamental reason for the exile, according to this passage?

_____

_____

_____

_____

_____

_____

What is the spiritual result of the Assyrian resettlement of Samaria as it is described in 17:24–41? Consider verses 29–33 especially.

_____

_____

_____

_____

_____

Read through the following three sections on *Gospel Glimpses*, *Whole-Bible Connections*, and *Theological Soundings*. Then take time to consider the *Personal Implications* these sections may have for you.

GOD'S COVENANT FAITHFULNESS. When Israel experiences oppression from Hazael of Syria, 2 Kings 13:23 notes, "The LORD was gracious to them and had compassion on them, and he turned toward them, because of his covenant with Abraham, Isaac, and Jacob, and would not destroy them, nor has he cast them from his presence until now." This is one of only a few instances in 1–2 Kings in which God's covenant faithfulness to his people is described specifically in terms of his promises to the patriarchs (Abraham, Isaac, and Jacob); more commonly, God's faithfulness is described in terms of the Davidic covenant and applied more directly to Judah (e.g., 1 Kings 8:22–26; 15:4–5; 2 Kings 8:19). Second Kings 13:23 indicates that God's commitment to his people, Israel and Judah alike, is ultimately deeper than the disruption of the exile. Since 1–2 Kings was written after the exile, the phrase "nor has he cast them from his presence until now" suggests that the exile is not the end of their story, for God has a deeper redemptive purpose stretching beyond the temporary chastisement of exile. The New Testament presents the coming of Christ as the ultimate fulfillment of God's covenant promises to the patriarchs (e.g., Luke 1:54–55, 73–74).

GOD'S COMPASSION FOR HIS PEOPLE. Second Kings 13:23 indicates that the motive behind God's protection of his people during the reign of Jehoahaz was his gracious compassion for them: "The LORD was gracious to them and had compassion on them, and he turned toward them." In 14:26–27, a similar motive is provided for God's protection of Israel under Jeroboam II: "The LORD saw that the affliction of Israel was very bitter, for there was none left, bond or free, and there was none to help Israel. But the LORD had not said that he would blot out the name of Israel from under heaven, so he saved them by the hand of Jeroboam the son of Joash." These verses remind us that even during relatively bleak times during the history of God's people, as they languish in idolatry under ungodly leadership, God remains true not only to his covenant promises but also to his gracious, compassionate character. Even in times of judgment and refining, God is unwilling to totally annihilate his people, not simply because of the formal obligations of covenant faithfulness but also because he genuinely pities them amid their affliction. During his earthly ministry, Christ also expressed pity for his people amid a time of judgment: "How often would I have gathered your children together as a hen gathers her brood under her wings, and you were not willing!" (Matt. 23:37).

JUDGMENT ON IDOLATRY. Second Kings 17:7–23 is a significant passage in the larger flow of 1–2 Kings, as the narrative pauses and the events are interpreted by the narrator. These verses describe the exile as the result of idolatry, recounting thoroughly the Israelites' forsaking their God and pursuing other gods, leading to their destruction. This emphasis on the destructive nature of idols corresponds to a larger pattern throughout Scripture showing how idols corrupt those who worship them. For example, 2 Kings 17:15 ("They went after false idols and became false") follows closely the logic of Psalm 115:8 ("Those who make [idols] become like them"), as well as the pervasive biblical emphasis on the futility of idol-making and idol worship (e.g., Isa. 44:9–11; Jer. 14:22; Hab. 2:18–29). In the New Testament, the apostle Paul depicts human unrighteousness in terms of worshiping created things in place of the Creator (Rom. 1:18–32).

EXILE. In 2 Kings 17, the people of the northern kingdom of Israel are taken into exile and scattered throughout various parts of the Assyrian Empire. The ultimate sting of exile, however, was not mere physical relocation but banishment from the presence and favor of God. Expulsion from the land of Israel represented a spiritual judgment because God had promised that his people would dwell in this place (e.g., Gen. 17:8). The motif of expulsion or exile from God's presence is the original judgment of sin at the fall of Adam and Eve, who were driven out of the garden of Eden for their disobedience (Gen. 3:24). On the cross, Jesus experienced the ultimate banishment from God's presence and favor as he bore the curse of sin for his people (Matt. 27:46), so that they would be restored to the blessing of access to God's presence (Heb. 10:19–22). We remain exiles in this world until Christ returns (1 Pet. 2:11), at which time we will once again enjoy unhindered access to the presence of God (Rev. 21:3).

▶ Theological Soundings

DIFFERING DEGREES OF FRUITFULNESS. This portion of Judah's history sees a series of kings who are basically good but are nonetheless ineffective in removing idolatry from among God's people: Jehoash, Amaziah, Azariah, and Jotham. They are described as doing what is right in the eyes of the Lord, but not like their father David; during their reigns they fail to remove the high places,[1] and most of them have a mixed legacy of accomplishments. There seems to be some doubt as to whether their obedience to the Lord is wholehearted. This portion of Scripture accords with others in teaching that, even among those inside the scope of God's grace, there can be differing levels of fruitfulness in service to the Lord (e.g., 1 Cor. 3:12–15).

RELIGIOUS SYNCRETISM.[2] When the king of Assyria brings people to resettle the land of Samaria in 2 Kings 17:29–41, he introduces many different expressions of foreign worship to the worship of the true God. But from the perspective of 2 Kings, worshiping the God of Israel alongside other gods is the same

72

as not worshiping him at all (see, e.g., 17:34). The narrator of 2 Kings attributes the religious syncretism and idolatry in Samaria at the time of the book's writing to the unfortunate consequence of this resettlement (2 Kings 17:34–41). This passage of Scripture accords with the rest of the Bible in affirming that the true God requires absolutely exclusive worship (e.g., Deut. 6:4–5).

> ## Personal Implications

Take time to reflect on the implications of 2 Kings 13–17 for your own life today. Make notes below on the personal implications for your walk with the Lord of the (1) *Gospel Glimpses*, (2) *Whole-Bible Connections*, (3) *Theological Soundings*, and (4) this passage as a whole.

1. Gospel Glimpses

2. Whole-Bible Connections

3. Theological Soundings

4. 2 Kings 13:1–17:41

As You Finish This Unit . . .

Take a moment now to ask for the Lord's blessing and help as you continue in this study of 2 Kings. And take a moment also to look back through this unit of study, to reflect on some key things that the Lord may be teaching you.

Definitions

[1] **High places** – Height may or may not have been a feature of these public sites where offerings were made to God or to false gods. Worshiping the Lord at a high place was legitimate before the time of the temple (1 Kings 3:2, 4). Later "high places," even those where the Lord was worshiped, were forbidden (2 Kings 23:15).

[2] **Syncretism** – A religious belief system that blends ideas and practices of various religions.

Week 10: Deliverance under Hezekiah, and Further Decline

2 Kings 18:1–21:26

The rise of Assyria is a threat not only to the northern kingdom of Israel but to Judah as well. The focus now turns south as King Hezekiah responds to the threat of attack from Assyria under Sennacherib. Judah is delivered from Assyria through Hezekiah's prayer and God's intervention (chs. 18–19), but Hezekiah's courtship of Babylon is an ominous portent (ch. 20). In chapter 21, the long reign of wicked Manasseh reverses the policies of his father, Hezekiah, and God's irreversible judgment on Judah is declared.

The Big Picture

God fulfills his promises to his people and brings salvation as they cry out to him in prayer.

Reflection and Discussion

Read through the complete passage for this study, 2 Kings 18–21. Then review the questions below concerning this section of 2 Kings and write your notes on them. (For further background, see the *ESV Study Bible*, pages 680–688; available online at esv.org.)

1. Assyria Attacks Judah (2 Kings 18)

Hezekiah is described as a righteous king who does what is right in the eyes of the Lord, "according to all that David his father had done" (18:3). In what specific ways in 2 Kings 18:1–6 do you see Hezekiah surpassing even the other good kings of Judah in his obedience to the Lord?

What do you think the words of the Rabshakeh[1] (vv. 19–35) are designed to make the Israelites *feel*? How does the Rabshakeh imply that trust in the Lord is as futile as trust in the gods of other nations?

2. The Lord Delivers Judah (2 Kings 19)

According to 2 Kings 19:1–8, how is God involved in the contest between Assyria and Judah? What attitude toward the God of Israel has been reflected in the words of the Rabshakeh?

When Hezekiah receives the threat from the king of Assyria, he goes to the temple to pray for deliverance (19:14–19). On what theological grounds does Hezekiah make his appeal to the Lord?

Isaiah's message to Hezekiah concerning the Assyrian king's downfall comes in three sections. First, he exposes and condemns Sennacherib's pride (vv. 21–28); second, he promises agricultural provision after the Assyrian withdrawal (vv. 29–31); third, he ensures the protection of Jerusalem from the Assyrian threat, grounded in God's commitment to the Davidic monarchy (vv. 32–34). What does Isaiah's prophecy reveal about God's character and his commitment to his people?

3. The Rest of Hezekiah's Rule (2 Kings 20)

In 20:1–11, Hezekiah is told by Isaiah that he will die, but the king cries out to the Lord and sees 15 years added to his life. Are there any indications in this passage that, despite his miraculous healing, Hezekiah's attitude is not fully pleasing to the Lord?

What do you think is Hezekiah's motive for showing the Babylonian envoys all of his treasure (20:12–13)? What attitude is reflected in his response to Isaiah's prophecy in verses 16–19?

3. Further Decline under Manasseh and Amon (2 Kings 21)

In 21:1–9, the sins of Manasseh are recounted. Manasseh is the very worst of the Judean kings, and his 55-year reign leads Judah into greater sin than had been committed by the nations the people of Israel had driven out of the land in the first place. According to verses 7–8, what effect did his rule have on the temple?

In 21:10–15, God declares utter devastation upon Judah and Jerusalem because of their sin, promising to deliver them into the hands of their enemies. How do the images used in these verses emphasize the horrific nature of this judgment? What do you think it would feel like to receive this prophecy?

Read through the following three sections on *Gospel Glimpses*, *Whole-Bible Connections*, and *Theological Soundings*. Then take time to consider the *Personal Implications* these sections may have for you.

Gospel Glimpses

GOD'S RESPONSIVENESS TO FAITH.[2] When Hezekiah hears the Assyrian threat, he goes to the temple of the Lord and cries out to God for deliverance: "Incline your ear, O LORD, and hear; open your eyes, O LORD, and see" (19:16). In response, God not only strikes down 185,000 of the Assyrian troops (and ultimately Sennacherib himself) but also gives Hezekiah personal assurance through the oracle of Isaiah the prophet. The purpose of Isaiah's prophecy, in part, is to relieve Hezekiah's fear (19:6–7) and assure him that "your prayer to me about Sennacherib king of Assyria I have heard" (19:20). This story emphasizes God's responsiveness to the faith of his people and his willingness to answer their prayers and deliver them from evil. All throughout his earthly ministry, Jesus showed this same responsiveness, frequently telling people, "According to your faith be it done to you" (e.g., Matt. 9:29).

GOD'S COMMITMENT TO THE DAVIDIC MONARCHY. Several times during Hezekiah's reign, God's deliverance of Jerusalem from the Assyrian army is cast in terms of God's faithfulness to the Davidic monarchy. In 2 Kings 19:34 and 20:6, God declares through the prophet Isaiah that he will save Jerusalem "for my own sake and for the sake of my servant David." These statements correspond to the hope articulated throughout 1–2 Kings that the Davidic monarchy would be preserved despite God's judgment on his people (1 Kings 11:13, 32–36; 15:4; 2 Kings 8:19). These statements situate God's salvation of Hezekiah and Jerusalem at this time in history within his larger purpose throughout all of redemptive history: to bring salvation to the entire world through the coming Davidic King, Jesus Christ.

Whole-Bible Connections

THE LORD ALONE IS GOD. When Hezekiah prays for deliverance from the Assyrian army, the stated purpose is not merely for Jerusalem's sake but so that "all the kingdoms of the earth may know that you, O LORD, are God alone" (2 Kings 19:19). This request echoes Solomon's request at the climax of his temple dedication prayer "that all the peoples of the earth may know that the LORD is God; there is no other" (1 Kings 8:60) and reflects the desire throughout the Bible for the true God to be seen in his unrivalled majesty and power, in contrast to false idols (see Deut. 6:4–5; John 17:3).

GOD CANNOT BE MOCKED. Second Kings devotes considerable space throughout chapters 18–19 to describing the taunts of the Rabshakeh. Ultimately, these taunts toward the people of Judah are interpreted as mocking and reviling the Lord himself (2 Kings 19:4, 6, 16, 21–22, 28). Isaiah's oracle, equally lengthy in response, serves to turn these taunts back onto the Assyrians: "She despises you, she scorns you; . . . she wags her head behind you" (19:21). Throughout the Bible, those who mock and oppose God find themselves in return being mocked and opposed by God. As Hannah prays, "The adversaries of the LORD shall be broken to pieces; against them he will thunder in heaven" (1 Sam. 2:10). As Psalm 2:1 asks, "Why do the nations rage and the peoples plot in vain?"

Theological Soundings

GOD'S SOVEREIGNTY. Isaiah's oracle against Sennacherib expresses astonishment at his arrogance and pride in defying the God of Israel: "Whom have you mocked and reviled? . . . The Holy One of Israel!" (19:22). In 19:25–26, Isaiah indicates the basis for this astonishment at Sennacherib's folly: his military accomplishments have not come about through his own strength or cunning but were sovereignly ordained by God long ago. Assyria is simply a tool in the hand of God to bring about his purposes of judgment, and the empire can be overturned at any time. Second Kings 19:25–26 accords with the rest of the Bible in affirming that God is sovereign over all events and is capable of using even evil to bring about his larger purposes (see Gen. 50:20; Acts 2:23).

IN WHOM DO YOU TRUST? Several times in his speech to the people of Judah, the Rabshakeh appeals to their ultimate sense of allegiance and trust: "On what do you rest this trust of yours? . . . In whom do you now trust?" (18:19–20). He declares that trusting the Lord is as futile as trusting Egypt (18:21–22) or the other pagan deities that have failed to stop the Assyrian conquest throughout the region (18:32–35; 19:11–13). Hezekiah's prayer reflects his understanding, in contrast to these Assyrian appeals, that the God of Israel is the true and living God: "O LORD, the God of Israel, enthroned above the cherubim, you are the God, you alone, of all the kingdoms of the earth; you have made heaven and earth" (19:15). Because God alone is the true God, he is worthy of our complete trust and allegiance, even when everything is on the line.

Personal Implications

Take time to reflect on the implications of 2 Kings 18–21 for your own life today. Make notes below on the personal implications for your walk with the Lord of the (1) *Gospel Glimpses*, (2) *Whole-Bible Connections*, (3) *Theological Soundings*, and (4) this passage as a whole.

1. Gospel Glimpses

2. Whole-Bible Connections

3. Theological Soundings

4. 2 Kings 18:1–21:26

> ## As You Finish This Unit . . .

Take a moment now to ask for the Lord's blessing and help as you continue in this study of 2 Kings. And take a moment also to look back through this unit of study, to reflect on some key things that the Lord may be teaching you.

Definitions

[1] **Rabshakeh** – The "chief cupbearer" and servant of the king, who in 2 Kings functions as a spokesperson on behalf of the Assyrian king and army.

[2] **Faith** – Trust in or reliance upon something or someone despite a lack of concrete proof. Salvation, which is purely a work of God's grace, can be received only through faith (Rom. 5:2; Eph. 2:8–9). The writer of Hebrews calls on believers to emulate those who lived godly lives by faith (Hebrews 11).

WEEK 11: REFORM UNDER JOSIAH AND THE FALL OF THE SOUTHERN KINGDOM

2 Kings 22:1–25:30

▲

The Place of the Passage

Hope returns to the story of Judah under the righteous leadership of Josiah, who leads the nation toward renewal and reform. But his efforts are not enough to avert disaster. Following the reigns of a few more unrighteous kings, the Babylonians lay siege to Jerusalem, destroy its temple, and deport the surviving residents. The story of 1–2 Kings thus comes to a tragic end, with only a glimmer of hope remaining in the survival of Jehoiachin, who was of the Davidic line (2 Kings 25:27–30).

The Big Picture

God brings judgment to his people for their sin and idolatry while sustaining hope for their future through the survival of the Davidic line.

> ## Reflection and Discussion

Read through the complete passage for this study, 2 Kings 22–25. Then review the questions below concerning this section of 2 Kings and write your notes on them. (For further background, see the *ESV Study Bible*, pages 688–695; available online at esv.org.)

1. Reforms under Josiah (2 Kings 22:1–23:30)

How is the Book of the Law[1] discovered during Josiah's reign? Why does its discovery provoke the reaction that it does from Josiah?

What does the Lord's response to Josiah in 22:14–20 reveal about Josiah's character? How do God's mercy and judgment relate to each other in this passage?

In 2 Kings 23, a number of Josiah's reforms are listed. First, in verses 1–3, Josiah calls together the elders of God's people at the temple to respond to God's Word in a covenant renewal ceremony. Then, in verses 4–20, he leads the nation in an extensive purging of various idolatrous institutions that had been established during Manasseh's reign. Third, in verses 21–23, he leads the nation in celebrating the Passover meal for the first time since the book of Judges. Finally, in a summary of his accomplishments in verses 24–25, we learn that he put away mediums and necromancers and other forms of idolatry sometimes associated with divination. What strikes you as the greatest of Josiah's accomplishments in this chapter? Why?

Despite all of Josiah's reforms, God declares that exile is still ordained for Judah (23:26–27). According to these verses, why are Josiah's reforms insufficient to avert this disaster?

2. The Final Kings of Judah (2 Kings 23:31–24:20)

The reigns of Jehoahaz, Jehoiakim, and Jehoiachin occur amid a power struggle between Egypt and Babylonia. Jehoahaz is taken captive by Pharaoh Neco of Egypt (23:31–35), and his brother and successor, Jehoiakim, becomes the servant of Nebuchadnezzar of Babylon (23:36–24:7). Jehoiakim's revolt causes the first siege of Jerusalem, resulting in a deportation in 597 BC. A decade later, King Zedekiah's revolt causes a second siege of Jerusalem and its final destruction (24:18–20; 25:1–22). As you read through the account of these events in 2 Kings, what theological interpretation do you find offered? Consider especially, for instance, 2 Kings 24:2–4, 20.

3. Judah Is Exiled (2 Kings 25)

Second Kings 25:1–7 recounts Babylon's final siege of Jerusalem, resulting ultimately in the slaughtering of Zedekiah's children before he is blinded and deported to Babylon. A few weeks later, in 25:8–17, the Babylonian army razes the city of Jerusalem, burning all of its important buildings and breaking down the city wall. Even the temple is destroyed and its valuable metal taken. Finally, in 25:18–21, a number of the leaders among God's people are taken back to Babylon and executed. This section ends with the summary statement, "So Judah was taken into exile out of its land" (25:21). What emotions does the narrative recounted in this section prompt in you as you read it? How would you have felt if you had lived through this horrific time?

Since God had promised that his presence would reside in the temple, what message is sent when the temple is destroyed? How is this event interpreted through earlier predictions in 2 Kings (e.g., 23:27; 24:20)?

What hope does it give the reader that 2 Kings ends with Jehoiachin's release from prison (25:27–30)? What is the significance of the book's ending in this way?

Read through the following three sections on *Gospel Glimpses*, *Whole-Bible Connections*, and *Theological Soundings*. Then take time to consider the *Personal Implications* these sections may have for you.

MERCY AMID JUDGMENT. This portion of Scripture is concerned greatly with God's judgment, which he has declared upon Judah for the sins of Manasseh, and which not even the righteous reign of Josiah can avert. Nonetheless, even while pledging his commitment to carry out his determined judgment (22:16–17; 23:26–27), God responds graciously to King Josiah "because your heart was penitent, and you humbled yourself before the LORD" (22:19). The story of righteous Josiah reminds us that God gives grace to all who respond to him with a penitent heart, no matter how dire the circumstances of life. It also reminds us that God's mercy and wrath are not to be pitted against one another; the Lord is capable of expressing mercy even amid larger purposes of judgment. As Habakkuk prayed, "In wrath remember mercy" (Hab. 3:2).

THE DAVIDIC LINE ENDURES. The books of 1–2 Kings end by describing the fate of the Judean king Jehoiachin, as Evil-Merodach of Babylonia (the son of Nebuchadnezzar) releases him from prison, speaks kindly to him, gives him a seat above the other kings in Babylon, and provides for his needs. This highlights God's faithfulness to the promise of the Davidic covenant of an everlasting kingdom for the line of David (2 Sam. 7:16). Throughout 1–2 Kings, the Davidic covenant is portrayed both as a conditional promise established through the obedience of various Davidic kings (e.g., 1 Kings 9:4–5) and as an unconditional promise that God will guarantee. Unlike that of Israel, the monarchy of Judah is unshakable; Jerusalem will always have a "lamp" before God (1 Kings 11:36; 2 Kings 8:19). The concluding postscript of 2 Kings regarding Jehoiachin's fate makes clear, however, that the unconditional aspect of the promise triumphs in the end; not even exile and temple destruction can extinguish the hope for a coming Davidic ruler. In the postexilic portion of the Old Testament, the divine appointment of Jehoiachin's great-grandson Zerubbabel (Hag. 2:23; compare Jer. 22:24–27) marks the reestablishment of the house of David; in the New Testament, Jesus Christ is installed on the Davidic throne upon his resurrection and ascension (see Rom. 1:1–4).

GOD'S REFORMING WORD. In 2 Kings 22 the Book of the Law is discovered, leading Josiah to tear his clothes in mourning (22:11) and to inquire of the Lord (22:12–13). In chapter 23, Josiah reads from the Book of the Law in order to initiate a covenant renewal ceremony (23:1–3), which leads to the purging of idolatry (23:4–20) and the restoration of the Passover[2] meal (23:21–23). Here, as throughout Scripture, God's Word is the initiating spark that leads to renewal and reformation among God's people. Throughout the Bible, it is God's Word to his people that initiates relationship with them and establishes their spiritual well-being—from God's speech to Adam in the garden of Eden (Gen. 2:16–17), to his various covenants with Noah (Gen. 6:13–22), Abraham (Gen. 12:1–3; 15:1–21; 17:1–27), Moses (Exodus 19–23), and David (2 Samuel 7), and to the restoration and covenant renewal of the prophets and postexilic leaders (Neh. 8:1–8; Isaiah 40). In the New Testament, God's kingdom is advanced as the Word of God is proclaimed (e.g., Acts 6:7, "The word of God continued to increase, and the number of the disciples multiplied greatly in Jerusalem"). The gospel message is often labeled "the word of the gospel" (Acts 15:7), "the word of his grace" (Acts 14:3), "the word of the cross" (1 Cor. 1:18), "the word of life" (Phil. 2:16), or "the word of truth" (James 1:18).

TEMPLE. In 2 Kings 25 the temple is razed and its furnishings carted off to Babylon. According to 2 Kings 23:27, this event represents God's judgment in casting off his people, removing them from his sight; according to 2 Kings 24:20, it is an expression of his anger and his desire to remove them from his presence. The destruction of the temple seemed to be the termination of a hope developing throughout the Bible that God would dwell among his people, initially represented by the garden of Eden and the tabernacle. But hope for a renewed temple soon develops (Ezekiel 40–48), and the postexilic books describe the rebuilding of the temple (Ezra, Haggai, Zechariah). In the New Testament, the incarnation of Jesus Christ is presented as God's "tabernacling" among us (John 1:14), and the hope is expressed that the people of God will one day enjoy the immediate dwelling of God among them (Rev. 21:3).

> ## Theological Soundings

THE PASSOVER MEAL. Josiah leads the people in 2 Kings 23:21–23 to celebrate the Passover meal for the first time since the time of the judges. Passover was instituted in Exodus 12:1–28 as a remembrance of God's deliverance of his people from the judgment that fell on the Egyptians, with further stipulations added in Deuteronomy 16:1–8. In the New Testament, the Lord's Supper is instituted during a Passover meal (Luke 22:15–20), leading many to see a connection between these two institutions. Paul identifies Jesus himself as the fulfillment of the lambs sacrificed at Passover (1 Cor. 5:7). Just as the blood of the lambs at the original sacrifice shielded the Israelites from judgment, so Christ's blood shields us, for it was shed on our behalf on the cross as Christ absorbed God's wrath for our sins.

DIVINE WRATH. The climax of 1–2 Kings is the judgment of exile, and much of 2 Kings 22–25 addresses God's commitment to bring about this judgment, as promised in 21:10–15 in response to Manasseh's idolatry, despite the reforming efforts of Josiah (e.g., 22:14–20; 23:26–27; 24:2–4, 20). The basis for God's judgment in several of these texts is his wrath, which has been "kindled" (22:17) against Judah and is "burning" (23:26) until it is quenched. While the doctrine of divine wrath is certainly a difficult one for many people to contemplate, it is presented in the Bible as the just and necessary response to evil and as one aspect of God's righteous character (see Nah. 1:2).

Personal Implications

Take time to reflect on the implications of 2 Kings 21–25 for your own life today. Make notes below on the personal implications for your walk with the Lord of the (1) *Gospel Glimpses*, (2) *Whole-Bible Connections*, (3) *Theological Soundings*, and (4) this passage as a whole.

1. Gospel Glimpses

2. Whole-Bible Connections

3. Theological Soundings

4. 2 Kings 22:1–25:30

As You Finish This Unit . . .

Take a moment now to ask for the Lord's blessing and help as you continue in this study of 2 Kings. And take a moment also to look back through this unit of study, to reflect on some key things that the Lord may be teaching you.

Definitions

[1] **The Book of the Law** – This phrase typically refers to the book of Deuteronomy (e.g., Deut. 31:26).

[2] **Passover meal** – An annual Israelite festival commemorating God's final plague on the Egyptians, which led to the exodus. In this final plague, the Lord "passed over" the houses of those who spread the blood of a lamb on the doorposts of their homes (Exodus 12). Those who did not obey this command suffered the death of their firstborn.

WEEK 12: SUMMARY AND CONCLUSION

We conclude our study of 1–2 Kings by summarizing the big picture of God's message through this book as a whole. Then we will consider several questions in order to reflect on various Gospel Glimpses, Whole-Bible Connections, and Theological Soundings throughout the entire book.

The Big Picture of 1–2 Kings

First and Second Kings bridge the period of Israel's history from David's reign to the exile. This is ultimately a tragic time, marked by disobedience, decline, and judgment. Yet 1–2 Kings also expresses hope that the exile is not the end of the story for God's redemptive purposes through and for his people.

The temple occupies a central role in the narrative of 1–2 Kings. Solomon's prayer of dedication in 1 Kings 8 is one the most theologically dense chapters in the entire Old Testament, and it is the destruction of the temple in 2 Kings 25 that, in large part, makes the Babylonian exile such a tragic event. The presence of the temple reflects God's desire to dwell among his people.

The primary spiritual struggle energizing 1–2 Kings is the conflict between idolatry and worship of the true God. It is in connection to this struggle that the ministries of various godly prophets take shape, especially those of Elijah and Elisha in combating Baal worship among God's people. A significant part of the message of 1–2 Kings is that there is only one true God, and he alone is worthy of worship and ultimate allegiance.

The great hope of 1–2 Kings is the Davidic covenant. The books are structured as a record of monarchical succession, and the preservation of the Davidic line is explicitly highlighted occasionally and is implicitly emphasized throughout. Several royal houses are utterly destroyed, such as those of Jeroboam and Ahab, but the Judean monarchy, established in Jerusalem, endures; even the disruption of the Babylonian exile does not extinguish this line (2 Kings 25:27–30). It is with this hope that 1–2 Kings ends, a hope that is also the primary way in which these books intersect with the larger biblical narrative.

Gospel Glimpses

The study of 1–2 Kings directs us to the gospel in numerous ways. Although the overall trajectory of the narrative leads to the tragic judgment of exile, there are abundant expressions of God's grace toward his people along the way. We think, for instance, of the wisdom and blessing bestowed upon Solomon, the faithful persistence of prophetic oracles among God's people (especially through the ministries of Elijah/Elisha), the miraculous answer to Hezekiah's prayer for deliverance, and God's responsiveness and favor toward the reform efforts of good Judean kings such as Jehoash and Josiah. Furthermore, God is faithful to maintain his promises to his people despite their disobedience, above all in the preservation of the Davidic line, even in exile.

Has 1–2 Kings brought new clarity to your understanding of the gospel? How so?

Were there any particular passages or themes in 1–2 Kings that led you to a fresh understanding and grasp of God's grace to us through Jesus?

▶ Whole-Bible Connections

Many larger biblical themes running from Genesis to Revelation are prominent in 1–2 Kings, and these books make a significant contribution to their development. The theme throughout the Bible of God's desire to dwell among his people would be woefully incomplete without the temple narrative of 1–2 Kings, at the start of which the temple is built and at the end of which the temple is utterly destroyed. The books of 1–2 Kings are the primary place in the Bible in which God's promise of the land of Canaan to his people, initiated with the patriarchs, is at least temporarily frustrated as disobedience leads to their expulsion from the land. Most significantly, 1–2 Kings evidences God's commitment to the Davidic covenant, as the Davidic line is preserved even through exile.

How has this study of 1–2 Kings filled out your understanding of the biblical storyline of redemption?

Are there any themes emphasized in 1–2 Kings that help you deepen your grasp of the Bible's unity?

Have any passages or themes expanded your understanding of the redemption that Jesus provides, begun at his first coming and to be consummated at his return?

What connections between 1–2 Kings and the New Testament were new to you?

Theological Soundings

First and Second Kings make a significant contribution to Christian theology. Many doctrines are developed, clarified, and reinforced throughout 1–2 Kings, such as God's judgment on idolatry, his covenant faithfulness to his people, the nature of prophecy and miracle, and the hope of the coming Davidic Messiah.

Has your own theology been refined during the course of studying 1–2 Kings? How so?

How has your understanding of the nature and character of God been deepened through this study?

What unique contributions does 1–2 Kings make toward our understanding of who Jesus is and what he accomplished through his life, death, and resurrection?

What specifically does 1–2 Kings teach us about the human condition and our need of redemption?

_____

_____

_____

_____

_____

_____

Personal Implications

God gave us 1–2 Kings, ultimately, to help us know and love him more deeply and walk more closely with him in our daily lives. As you reflect on 1–2 Kings as a whole, what implications do you see for your own life?

_____

_____

_____

_____

_____

_____

What life implications flow from your reflections on the questions already asked in this week's study concerning Gospel Glimpses, Whole-Bible Connections, and Theological Soundings?

_____

_____

_____

_____

_____

_____

What has 1–2 Kings brought home to you that leads you to praise God, turn away from sin, and trust more firmly in his promises?

_____

_____

_____

_____

_____

_____

▶ As You Finish Studying 1–2 Kings . . .

We rejoice with you as you finish studying 1–2 Kings! May this study become part of your Christian walk of faith, day by day and week by week throughout all your life. Now we would greatly encourage you to study the Word of God in an ongoing way. To help you as you continue your study of the Bible, we would encourage you to consider other books in the *Knowing the Bible* series, and to visit www.knowingthebibleseries.org.

Lastly, take a moment to look back through this study. Review the notes that you have written, and the things that you have highlighted or underlined. Reflect again on the key themes that the Lord has been teaching you about himself and about his Word. May these things become a treasure for you throughout your life—which we pray will be true for you, in the name of the Father, and the Son, and the Holy Spirit. Amen.